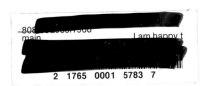

T3-AKD-728

I AM HAPPY TO PRESENT

SECOND EDITION

I Am Happy to Present

A BOOK OF INTRODUCTIONS

COMPILED BY

Guy R. Lyle and Kevin Guinagh

THE H. W. WILSON COMPANY · NEW YORK 1968

PREFACE

To the Second Edition

SOMEONE HAS SAID that the function of an emcee in relation to a speaker is like that of a fan to a fan dancer; it calls attention to the subject but makes no attempt to cover it. The compilers of this book feel the same way about the preface to a book. Accordingly, we shall say simply that we are pleased that this work has proved its usefulness by the demand for a new edition. It has been brought up to date by the deletion of twenty-three introductions in the first edition and the addition of forty-three new introductions.

For those who are unfamiliar with the first edition, it consisted of a collection of eighty-six introductory speeches selected from many sources, preceded by a brief, and we hope, suggestive essay on the art and method of making introductions. In reviewing the first edition, the distinguished bookman and book reviewer John T. Frederick wrote: "Most of us, every so often, are called upon to make a speech or to introduce someone else who is going to make one; and even though we may have done it a good many times before, we are likely to wish for help, for some way of doing it better. We can find such help in . . . *I Am Happy to Present*." To this succinct statement of purpose we would simply add that we have thought of the introduction as a literary genre which has entertainment value in its own right, and that we have at all times kept the general reader in mind.

A short list of acknowledgments is appended. This is not intended to supersede that in the first edition, but rather to supplement it by calling attention to the sources and permissions granted for the selections added to the second edition.

SEPTEMBER 1967

v

CONTENTS

THE LAW

THE MILITARY

RELIGION AND SOCIAL WORK

THE ARTFUL

INTRODUCTION

THE ARTFUL INTRODUCTION

So, you have to make a speech!

A month ago you were asked to make a few remarks to introduce a visiting speaker. Now the unhoped-for day is riding down upon you; you must brace yourself for the ordeal. The chairman of the program committee telephones to say that the speaker will arrive in plenty of time for you to make his acquaintance, or perhaps the word has reached you that the beeves and fatlings have already been killed for the banquet where you are to say "a few words." You must go through with it; you cannot escape.

Unless you are one of those who make their living by talking, as lawyers, ministers, and teachers do, you may begin to walk the floor, to bite your nails, to wake up at four in a cold sweat. However, this is the hour for resolution. If you start working immediately, you will be able to get hold of yourself; if you continue worrying, the date of your engagement may be the day when they take you to the hospital.

Really you have nothing to worry about. If that seems an exaggeration, let us say with Franklin Roosevelt that you have nothing to fear but fear. You may yet be a great success in spite of your fears, whereas many who have been making speeches for years and who feel they need no preparation may turn in a very poor performance in spite of their confidence. They are really unteachable, though there is much that they might learn.

What you are called upon to do is not at all unusual. Thousands of your fellow Americans in the course of a day are called upon to address Rotary, Kiwanis, Lions Clubs; church organizations, parent-teacher associations, athletic teams being feted after victory; political rallies, fund raising campaigns, civic improvement meetings; cultural, business, and professional groups. These speakers all seem to survive the trial of opening the mouth in public, and there is no reason why you should not be as fortunate. You are not alone.

But still you are worried about your speech. You talk the matter over with your wife, or *mutatis mutandis,* with your husband, and you derive little comfort from the counsel you receive.

"But, dear," your spouse will say, "you don't have to make a speech. All you have to do is to introduce the speaker of the evening."

For such remarks the stony stare and the short snort were invented.

Of course, she is only trying to build you up, to give you the confidence you need. Not being an expert in psychology, she thinks she can set your mind at ease by impatiently denying the obvious.

IMPORTANCE OF THE INTRODUCTION

Our social conventions require that a guest speaker be properly presented to his audience. While this is not absolutely necessary, still it may have much to do with the success of the meeting. What you are called upon to do is important. It is your business to put the audience in the proper mood for the speaker by presenting him in a favorable light. You are to give tone to the meeting, which can be as important as giving a violinist the note by which he tunes his instrument.

Because it is awkward and embarrassing for a man to rise and say, "I am Mr. So-and-So from Chicago, and I propose to address you on 'The Problems of a Great City,' " someone who is acquainted with the speaker's career should step forward and tell something of his background and why he is entitled to discuss the subject of the lecture. The audience will invariably be interested in how he gained his fame, the difficulties he encountered in achieving his reputation, the positions he has held, and the honors that have been conferred on him. Many in the audience will know little of the background of the visitor, and generally nobody will be acquainted with all his claims to a hearing.

BE BRIEF

You must keep in mind that you are not the main attraction of the meeting; you are the *hors d'œuvre,* not the *pièce de résistance,* the appetizer, not the main course. People have paid money or have given up their leisure to hear a speaker of some prominence who is to entertain, move, or inform them. They become impatient if the pleasure of hearing him is delayed. It tires an audience if you take too much time to present a speaker, as people weary of hearing about Christmas when the merchants begin warning us of its approach the day after Thanksgiving. Listeners have a certain amount of attention they can give a public speaker, generally not much more than an hour, unless he is exceptionally interesting. If you take twenty minutes to introduce him, you rob the speaker of his time and the audience of the price of admission.

Men in whom the platform manner is ingrained seem to find it impossible to limit their remarks to five minutes; there is a certain development their thoughts must take and this cannot be hastened. Some must pace the ages and go back several centuries to get a running start, often to the garden of Eden, to show how it was with Adam and Eve. It frequently happens that some preliminary speaker takes so long to give his little announcements that when the time comes for the principal speaker, he must race through his paper, reading only parts of it because the meeting must adjourn at a definite hour.

Chief Justice Taft once called attention to this impulse of a preliminary speaker to hold the spotlight, and dealt a rough rebuke to the offender. Mr. Taft was chairman of the meeting at which several persons of distinction were to speak for only five minutes each. A young man, charged with delivering some preliminary remarks, held the floor for three quarters of an hour before he was ready to yield. Mr. Taft, who had seen this happen before, rose when the orator finally finished and recalled a similar occasion when a preliminary speaker, after holding the platform unreasonably long, announced that the visitor of the evening would now give his address. Thereupon the gentleman stepped forward and rather testily gave his home address in New York City, adding that he was going there at once on a train that was leaving in fifteen minutes.

But Not Too Brief!

Some introducers go to the opposite extreme and give only a few seconds to the task of presenting a speaker to an audience. This is proper when the speaker is known to everybody, as in the case of the President of the United States, who is properly presented with the simple statement: "Ladies and Gentlemen, the President of the United States." However, in introducing a much less known personality, such brevity is inexcusable, since it may indicate a lack of personal warmth for the speaker. One of the old-time shoolmen of the Midwest invariably introduced speakers with the same sentence: "I have the honor to present Mr. So-and-So who will speak on such matters and at such length as he pleases." This is an easy way out for a lazy chairman, but it is hardly cordial to the speaker. Moreover, the attention of the audience might be heightened if some facts concerning his reputation and experience were given before the speech. Certainly the audience will be put in a receptive frame of mind by the suggestion that the speaker is a man of some reputation and an authority on the subject he is about to discuss.

On rare occasions the presentation of an important personality may last fifteen minutes. This is permissible when the introducer is himself able and distinguished. An example of such an introduction is the one given British Ambassador James Bryce by Joseph H. Choate (pages 237–41). In spite of its length this was well received, and the speaker was frequently interrupted by laughter and applause. Too often, however, introductions as long as this one are rambling, repetitive, and boring, and create the impression that the person making the presentation has an appetite for displaying his talents, whether real or fancied.

Talk About the Speaker, Not Yourself

The focus of attention should be the speaker and it is your business to throw the spotlight on him. Too frequently the introducer forgets that he is to acquaint the audience with the speaker, not with himself. The introducer may be the better man of the two, with a much better speech on the tip of his tongue, with experience and knowledge surpassing that of the visitor, but the audience has not come to hear the introducer but the stranger. It is an offense against good taste to try to call attention to oneself when the assigned chore is clearly that of presenting another. At times it is hardly possible to avoid casual mention of oneself, as, for example, if one were to recall the first time he met the speaker or heard his work mentioned. However, such a reference should reflect credit on the speaker. As an instance of the grace with which a personal reference can be made in such matters, read Sir Owen Seaman's introduction of Stephen Leacock to a London audience (pages 47–48).

Should You Be Reminded of a Joke?

Should the present occasion always bring to your mind a story or a joke? In the first place, can you tell a joke? If you can't, don't. How are you to know if you can or can't, you ask? It shouldn't be difficult to determine your skill in this matter. When you tell a story, do people laugh politely or not at all? or do they laugh naturally, sometimes uncontrollably? But you say that your type of humor is more subtle and does not call for laughter. Well, then, do people ever say hurriedly: "I've heard that one"? Do they try to change the subject? Do you find yourself telling the climax of your story to a different person from the one to whom you began telling it? Are you ever asked to repeat a story? If your answer to these questions is encouraging, it may well be that you are in the tradition of Nye, Ward, Twain, Leacock, Benchley, and Jessel. But precisely because you have a talent for wit you must remember that your great mistake may be that you joke on every occasion, that you can never play your role straight. If you tell a joke well, you must use great judgment in selecting the proper story and not run the risk of offending the speaker simply to raise a laugh.

If, for example, the Parent-Teacher Association asks you to introduce a physician who is to speak on "Respiratory Diseases in Children," this is not the time to be reminded of your story of the doctor who took out the patient's appendix instead of his tonsils. Some of the healthy unimpressionable fathers in the audience will laugh, but the judicious will weep while some of the sensitive mothers may become indignant and ask what punishment the offending doctor received. Nor does a professor who is set to talk on "The Symptoms of Inflation" relish a story on the absent-mindedness of professors. Imagine how the learned gentleman will feel, if you present him in this way:

The gentleman who is to speak to you is a professor, and so I am reminded of a story about the absent-mindedness of professors. Once three of them were sitting in a bus terminal, waiting for a bus to come in. They were busy thinking and talking, and failed to realize that their bus was in the station until it was already leaving. They made a wild dash for it and two of them succeeded in getting on.

The station attendant tried to console the man left behind. "Well," he said sympathetically, "two of you made it anyway."

"Yes," said the professor who was left behind, "but they just came down to see me off."

And now, Professor, we want to congratulate you on not missing the bus this evening. Ladies and gentlemen, I give you Professor So-and-So, who will discuss "The Symptoms of Inflation."

The learned professor will be pardoned for privately feeling that it were better if you had never been born.

Should You Write What You Are Going to Say?

If you do not have well in mind what you are going to say, it is a very good practice to work out your thoughts on paper. Try several different approaches. After you have written yourself empty — which may be preceded by reading yourself full — you can select the best you have.

It is difficult to persuade some people of the importance of writing out what they are going to say. They contend that they never have broken down in their lives and boast they never will; they never have to stop for a word. As a matter of fact, they never stop to think, but run the risk of saying the first thing that comes to mind, and this they may regret for years. The trouble with speaking without preparation is that you run into a trap before you realize it, and from this trap there is no escaping.

But you may object that writing is very difficult for you. Be frank and admit that you have no ideas. If you did, you would find the words to express them. Get hold of the matter and the words will follow, runs the ancient saw. What really is bothering you is that you don't know what to say. If you go over the news reporter's checklist of circumstances — who, what, where, by whose aid, why, how, and when — you will find that your problem is one of selecting the best from many points you can bring out. If you have the answers to these questions, none of the important vital statistics of the speaker's life will be forgotten. A little brooding over the material will bring out some unifying idea that can be developed artistically.

After you have settled on the ideas you intend to include in your introduction, list the points you intend to make. Generally this is preferable to memorizing what you have to say, for the reason that it is extremely difficult to avoid giving the impression that you are reciting a lesson learnt for school. Some men with great facility in memorizing — William Jennings Bryan was one of these — are able to speak their piece with such ease as to give the impression that they are speaking extemporaneously, but they are very rare.

So brief a performance as an introduction should not be read, though some notes may be permissible if you intend to enumerate the honors that have come to the speaker. To read an introduction verbatim argues excessive caution or little native wit. Some unkind critics may say that your wife must have written it for you.

Be Natural

It is a mistake to speak in a style that is alien to your natural manner. Talk in your own simple way and avoid a florid, bombastic style, so dear to the heart of the old-school politician. When a child of the present generation talks in this manner, listeners will conclude that he is repeating something he has read in a book. This excessively florid style runs to metaphors, which easily become mixed when the extemporaneous speaker lets his thoughts run like a herd in wild abandon. Generally such comparisons are exaggerations and are understood as such, but when the object to which a person is compared is credited with powers beyond its nature, language runs amuck. Thus a man may be introduced as a lion in the battle against whatever party may be in power. When the speaker begins to give qualities to the lion that are not leonine, a mixed metaphor results, as in the following:

Our speaker this evening has been a lion in the battle against the opposition, a lion that will open the door to a new horizon where the ship of state will become a whip to crush the forces of corruption.

If this is uttered with enough enthusiasm, there will be considerable applause, for the scrambling of metaphors may not disturb many of the listeners. But such a speaker is riding for an eventual fall.

When we say that one should speak in his natural manner, it is not meant that a person who has difficulties with grammar or pronunciation in ordinary speech should unabashedly go ahead and make those errors in material which he has had a chance to prepare. In every audience there will be many hearers who will recognize mistakes involving the objective case, the dangling participle, the wrong agreement between subject and predicate. If you are not conscious of these errors but know that your grammar is faulty, you must ask a friend to check your manuscript before you begin to memorize.

Do Not Overpraise

Do not overpraise the person you are introducing. Few people really object to a little praise in spite of their disclaimers and their affected modesty. Actually, speakers know that they have talent and do not object to having it revealed. But do not overdo it. Stick to the facts. When achievements are overstated and comparisons made with other notables in the field, a genuinely modest man will become uncomfortable and squirm publicly, especially if there are those present who are aware of his limitations. Instead of helping the speaker, you are embarrassing and distracting him.

Horatio Alger, the author of many juvenile stories written according to the rags-to-riches formula, was once called upon to address a group of New York newsboys. A certain Charles O'Connor gave him a very flowery introduction. At the time, Harrison and Cleveland were campaigning for the presidency of the United States. O'Connor pointed out that although Alger did not seek the presidency, it was not beyond the realm of possibility in his case. When Alger began to speak he felt smothered by these superlatives and was distracted by the hitherto unconsidered possibility that he was presidential material. Because of this introduction he gave a rather poor speech.

If the introduction is too elaborate and the visitor's performance far short of what you promised it would be, you will share the unpopularity of the speaker.

DON'T BELITTLE OR PATRONIZE

Equally graceless is the belittling, patronizing tone. The introducer, unwilling to jeopardize his own reputation by identifying himself with the unknown visitor, may avoid mentioning him and discourse sagely on the possibilities in the theme the speaker has chosen. He may point out its peculiar timeliness and amplify his point by stating that one can scarcely pick up a daily, a weekly, a monthly — nay, even a quarterly — that does not discuss the subject in great detail. Men are arguing about it in the factories, restaurants, clubs, bars, and poolrooms. Everybody has his own opinion on the matter, from senators and college presidents down to the laborers in the ditch and the paper boys on the corner. The speaker of the evening will attempt to throw a little light on this vexing subject. He is a younger man. The introducer has not heard the speech and does not know where the visitor will take his stand, but he does know from the advance publicity sent on by the press agent that there are people not without some reputation who have gone on record as approving the speaker's point of view. Then the introducer says that it gives him great pleasure to present the speaker of the evening.

The preliminary speaker has completely failed in what he was supposed to do. Instead of encouraging the speaker and making him feel that he is among friends, the introducer starts him off with a definite handicap, giving the impression that the subject to be discussed is trite and the visitor just one of thousands who could handle the theme.

It is evident that such an introducer is unprepared. He has not looked up the facts and consequently knows nothing of the speaker's education or experience; so, he saves face by climbing on a pedestal. He calls the speaker a young man, which is a compliment if one is applying for admission to the military service or contemplating marriage or fighting for a place on the varsity team; but when a speaker is moistening his lips preparatory to giving his speech, it is a definite setback. Even a lady being introduced in such circumstances will not be pleased to be referred to as young. As a public speaker, she will be interested in instructing or persuading, and the mention of her youth will carry with it the suggestion of immaturity.

It's Good to Be on Edge

In spite of earnest preparation, you may suffer from stage fright. This may not be of the advanced type, causing your knees to shake and your tongue to become so dry that you cannot moisten your lips, but you may suffer from a pronounced apprehension or a gnawing worry as the hour of your appearance approaches. This will disappear, once you begin to speak.

Actually it is better when speaking in public to be a little on edge. The accelerated pulse brings a speaker to life, helps his concentration, gives the impression that he is enthusiastic about his subject; whereas the speaker who is completely calm and undisturbed may be a perfect master of the situation but he runs the risk of being regarded by many as dull, colorless, and uninteresting.

Helping the Speaker

The spirit in which a speaker is handled may have much to do with the success of his speech. If he has been well treated before the meeting, he will sense that he is among friends and will make an unusual effort to please. He may be inspired by the occasion and the treatment accorded him. If, however, nobody is on hand to meet him, if he must find his own accommodations, take his chances with local restaurants, and get in touch with you or the chairman of the committee, he is likely not to do his best. Then, if in your introduction you tell him how happy you are to see him, how happy to welcome him to your city and organization, he will know that you are insincere. Your best effort may fail to establish a happy mood in the speaker's mind.

Occasionally at a banquet the introducer rises to make his remarks before the tables are cleared, thinking that by the time he has finished, there will be quiet in the hall, but often the speaker of the evening finds himself competing with the noise of bustling waiters and clashing dishes, which at times continues in an adjoining kitchen where pots and pans are being washed. This is very distracting to the speaker and the audience alike. At other types of meetings, midway in the speech of the evening, a number of ladies will begin moving about very noiselessly on tiptoe. They are preparing the refreshments to be served later. If you can control such ill-timed activities, you should.

Presenting this Book

In the following pages you will find a great many examples of this neglected literary genre suitable for a great variety of occasions. Here you may read introductions given by such masters of the art as Samuel L. Clemens, William Lyon Phelps, Chauncey Depew, Louis Nizer, and George Jessel. We have turned over a large library to find them, but they are doubtless not the finest that have ever been given, for many of the best have been extemporaneous and unrecorded, or if written down have been cast aside by their authors as trivial. Sometimes these pieces are better than the speeches that follow them.

It is not intended that those here collected should be used in their entirety by anyone faced with the problem of chairing a meeting, but these examples may serve to stimulate your own thoughts, to set your own ideas in motion when you note in what others have said parallels to the occasion for which you are preparing. Of course, what one needs most when called upon to speak in public is a residue of culture that has been accumulating for years. This is the product of reflection, good judgment, and esthetic feeling. Men and women who have been reading the right books, who have been trying to develop moral convictions and esthetic judgments, will wedge some of this into what they say. Even though they have had little experience in facing an audience, they may in their early efforts surpass many who have by reason of their position been raising their voices in public for years.

THE ARTS

Louis Nizer presents

George Gershwin

George Gershwin (1898–1937), the pianist and composer of musical comedy songs and orchestral works, is here introduced by Louis Nizer, prominent New York lawyer, whose fascinating book of courtroom stories and tactics, *My Life in Court*, was published in 1961.

THE CHINESE ascribed music to supernatural beings. We, who believe that man was made in the image of God, know that God's voice is represented by music.

It is generally thought that George Gershwin wrote his *Rhapsody in Blue* in three weeks. He believes so too. But he is mistaken. He wrote it during every second of his life. That which a composer creates is the result of mysterious processes upon his experiences.

Gershwin wrote the *Rhapsody* when he whistled his way through the East Side ghetto to a school on Rivington Street.

He wrote it when he was a song plugger for Remick at fifteen dollars a week.

He wrote it when, at the age of twenty, he composed his first musical comedy score, *La La Lucille*.

He wrote it when he composed the musical comedies *Our Nell* and *George White's Scandals*.

He wrote it when he composed "Swanee" and its two million copies carried his strains to fifty million ears.

Most aspiring composers obtain musical educations in order that they may give proper scope to their latent talents. When preparation has been completed they apply their training to their creativeness.

Gershwin has violated this rule. He possessed and expressed an enormous talent before he educated himself. At the age of ten he took some piano lessons from a musician whose only resemblance to Beethoven was his deafness. The charge was only twenty-five cents a lesson because the teacher could not hear the mistakes. Later he studied harmony under Rubin Goldmark. After six months he brought to his teacher a movement for a string quartet which he had composed before he began his studies. The master examined it and said, "This shows what amazing progress you have made since you began the study of harmony." His understanding of music was deeper than the rules could probe.

After Gershwin became famous he decided that he owed it to his talent to educate it. Thus he reversed the process. He proceeded from achievement to study, not from study to achievement.

This is as it should be in music. The technical rules often becloud the natural music. Franz Schubert took his first lesson in counterpoint one year before he died. Prior to his studies he had permanently enriched the world with melodies that flowed from inner sources beyond the reach of instruction.

Walter Damrosch has rightly said that Gershwin made a lady of jazz. Critics used to frown upon it as music which people heard through their feet instead of their brains. But Gershwin has applied jazz to larger symphonic forms. He has made it speak a more poignant message. Ravel, Kurt Weill, and Igor Stravinsky have adopted it.

Isaak Walton might have foreseen Gershwin when he exclaimed, "Lord, what music hast thou provided for the saints in heaven, when thou affordest bad men such music on earth?" Yes, such music as *Porgy and Bess, Concerto in F, American in Paris,* and his countless melodies. Even bad men deserve good music, for it is the only sensual pleasure without vice.

And yet, in a certain sense, no composer originates music. He merely reminds us of feelings which lie latent, but are ever ready for awakening.

I present to you the great reminder, who agitates fathomless depths and evokes the mysteries of the past within us.

Ladies and Gentlemen — George Gershwin!

Thomas R. Mulroy presents Ilka Chase

Thomas R. Mulroy, Chicago attorney, introduced Ilka Chase, radio, stage, and screen star, as the feature speaker at the April 21, 1944, meeting of the Executives' Club of Chicago.

IT IS A tradition of this club, Miss Chase, that the president in introducing an artiste such as you must attempt to be satiric and sardonic — but not today! You, my dear lady, are a dangerous woman, and I would not think of letting you have the last laugh.

You know, there is an old adage that God made women without a sense of humor so that they could love men instead of laughing at them. Our guest is a devastating exception to that rule.

Anyway, it is too hard to introduce women. You have to select your words with such infinite care. For example, you may call a woman a kitten, but you must not call her a cat.

You may call a woman a mouse, but definitely not a rat!

You may call a woman, as a term of endearment, "duck," but you simply must avoid "goose!"

You may, and I recommend it to you gentlemen, greet your wife in the morning with a cheery: "My dear, you certainly are a vision," but, please, oh, please, never say, "My dear, you certainly are a sight!"

Miss Chase is a fashion expert. She has exquisite taste, always knowing the right thing to wear at the right time. Not so, all women. I was in Florida this winter and all the slacks I saw on women reminded me of the Lucky Strike advertisement: "So round, so firm, so fully packed!"

But men are queer, too. They say the main difference between man and beast is man's brains, but there the difference ends, because man is lion-hearted, chicken-livered, pigeon-toed, busy as a bee, sly as a fox, blind as a bat, gentle as a lamb, drunk as a hoot owl, stubborn as a mule, strong as an ox, vain as a peacock, happy as a lark, or crazy as a loon — depending upon your particular point of view.

17

Miss Chase gained stage fame on Broadway by her portrayal of the part of the brazen cat, and I don't mean kitten, in the play entitled *The Women*. She is now a scintillating movie star.

Miss Chase is the author of two successive best sellers, *Past Imperfect* and *In Bed We Cry*. I read *Past Imperfect* and liked it very much. I read *In Bed We Cry* . . . period!!

Abraham Lincoln once wrote a review of a book — not Miss Chase's, of course — from which I wonder if I might adopt his comments as my own view of *In Bed We Cry*. Mr. Lincoln wrote:

"For those who like this kind of book, this is the kind of a book they will like."

Miss Chase has always been years ahead of her time, a genuine prodigy.

At the tender age of fourteen, she was valedictorian of her graduating class in a secluded convent school, and on the occasion of her address she delivered this sweet, idealistic, and unsophisticated philosophy of true love (with my own apologies to Dorothy Parker):

Dear fathers, mothers, and classmates, I would like to recite a poem about true love:

> When you finally swear you're his,
> Shivering and sighing,
> And he vows his passion is
> Infinite, undying, —
> Classmates, make a note of this:
> One of you is lying!

Here is indeed the truly soft-spoken woman's woman, incorrigible romanticist, shy rosebud, as we next find her at the age of twenty-five. One evening an old friend of the family rushed in to her and said, sobbing: "Ilka, some man has taken my car and run away with my wife!"

"No! No!" exclaimed Ilka, "Not your *new* car!"

Now that all my bad jokes are concluded let me say in all earnestness that this huge gathering today is a dramatic tribute to Ilka Chase, one of America's brilliant women.

I do now present to you, with a genuine feeling of privilege, the one and only Ilka Chase.

Deems Taylor presents
Grace George

This is an example of an introduction not of a speaker but of the winner of an award of the Medal for Good Speech on the Stage. The presentation to Miss George was made by Deems Taylor, distinguished American composer, author, and music critic, on the occasion of the joint ceremonial of the American Academy of Arts and Letters and the National Institute of Arts and Letters, May 25, 1950.

WHENEVER a group gathers to pay tribute to someone of the theatre, particularly to an actress, the spokesman for the group seems to feel it incumbent upon him to announce that he has been an ardent admirer of hers ever since he first saw her, as a tiny little boy. I venture to defy that compulsion. When I first saw Grace George, in *Divorçons*, I was *not* led into the theatre by my dear old French governess. To tell the truth, at the time that play was running at Wallack's Theatre, I was engaged in the dreary task of reading proof in an encyclopedia office. I offer this faintly gratuitous autobiographical titbit merely to establish the fact that I speak today as a reasonable facsimile of one of her contemporaries. Furthermore, being fresh out of college, I was a much severer and more confident authority on matters pertaining to the theatre than I am today. So that when, following my private discovery of Miss George's talents, I announced that she was magnificent, I was not so much expressing an opinion as stating a fact. And, so far as I am concerned, that fact, stated forty-three years ago, remains a fact today. She *is* magnificent.

Statistics make dull reading, and even duller hearing. So I shall not go into detail in summarizing Grace George's career. Suffice it to say that, after having achieved the rare distinction of being born in New York City, she graduated from a New Jersey convent school and the American Academy of Dramatic Arts, and made her first appearance on the American stage at the age of fifteen, in a play entitled *The New Boy* — which might better have been called "The New Girl." Of her subsequent career I have time to give you only a few reminders. Among the many, many plays in which she has starred are *Divorçons,* which introduced her to me and to London; *The School for Scandal; Much Ado About Nothing; Major Barbara* — which she introduced to America; *Captain Brassbound's Conversion* and *The Legend of Leonora. The Velvet Glove,* in which Miss George has just completed a twenty weeks' engagement, is her *sixtieth* play.

As a matter of fact, we are not here today, primarily, to hail her as an actress. That has been done by many organizations and many people, for many years. The Drama League of New York has just honored itself by giving her the Drama League Award for the most distinguished performance of the year. So, for a moment, suppose we take Grace George, the actress, for granted, while I explain why we have asked her to be with us today.

It is a great pity that here in America we have no official standard for the pronunciation and delivery of our native language. Other countries do better. In France, for example, the official pronunciation of the French language is the language heard upon the stage of the national theatre, the Comédie Française. Its actors come from all parts of France, and presumably speak with many regional accents. But once they join that company they speak, or must learn to speak, the language of the Comédie. And that language is the standard by which the correctness of a Frenchman's speech is judged.

Here we have no such standard, or, at least, no official one. Our people speak with many accents — Boston, Southern, Middle West, Texas, Far West. They are pleasant enough to hear, and have a charm of their own. But you cannot say that any one of them is authentic American English. And so, if we are to have any standard of good speech, we must look to a medium that is heard by many people. And that medium, as in France, should be the theatre. And don't underestimate the size of its audience. A play that has a good run will be heard by half a million people. It is true that there are other media that command a much larger audience: the radio, motion pictures, and now, television. Unfortunately, they are not wholly trust-worthy guides. The English they offer us is just as often bad English as good English. And so the responsibility for setting an example of good speech rests on the American actor even more heavily than in the past. Today we pay tribute to one who has brilliantly met that responsibility. From the earliest years of her career, Grace George has spoken an American English that is flawless in its clarity, intelligibility, and purity.

Therefore, Miss George, it is with pride and gratitude that we offer you the Medal of the American Academy of Arts and Letters for Good Speech on the Stage . . . and high time, too.

G. Lynn Sumner presents
Gertrude Lawrence

The actress Gertrude Lawrence (1898–1952) was introduced at a celebrity luncheon of the Advertising Club of New York, November 2, 1939. She was at the time starring with Donald Cook in John Golden's *Skylark*. The presiding officer was G. Lynn Sumner, president of the Advertising Club at that time.

IT IS A traditional example of the busman's holiday that when a sailor gets a day's shore leave, he goes rowing in Central Park. And if you would know what advertising men are doing these autumn nights — well, they are flocking to the Morosco Theatre, where some aspects of the advertising business have been cleverly put into a play called *Skylark*. The scintillating star of that play — Miss Gertrude Lawrence — is our special guest of honor today. That is the reason why we had no trouble whatever getting a complete set of our vice presidents at the head table.

In *Skylark*, Miss Lawrence plays a familiar part — the neglected wife of an advertising agency executive who is so busy with his clients and his speculative plans for prospective clients that he too often forgets to come home. Of course this is just a play — just a comedy — all in fun — for I am very sure that if Miss Lawrence were *really* the wife of an advertising agency executive, his chief problem would be to keep his mind on his work.

From observation of her theatre audiences, supplemented by observations of this audience, Miss Lawrence has some observations of her own to make about advertising and advertising men. I hope she doesn't pull her punches. It is a great pleasure to present one of the most charming and talented actresses of the English and American stage — Miss Gertrude Lawrence.

Thomas W. Lamont presents
Eleanor Robson Belmont

A leading actress before her marriage, Eleanor Robson Belmont (Mrs. August Belmont) was active in Red Cross work during World War I, and for many years served as an official of the Metropolitan Opera Association. She was presented with the medal of the National Institute of Social Sciences at its annual dinner May 10, 1934, and was introduced on this occasion by Thomas W. Lamont, partner of J. P. Morgan and Company.

THE MEMBERS of this Institute would never expect me to make a formal address in regard to a person like Mrs. Belmont, whose activities and works have always moved along lines not of formality but of real life. Further, I must not be too apologetic for the task that has been conferred upon me, but I must confess that it is not too easy to say or to attempt to say the correct thing for one whom I have so long claimed as a personal friend. If I say too much I slop over; if I say too little I become very formal. In fact, I almost remind myself of that salesman in a shoe shop in London who said to a woman customer of his, "I am sorry, Madam, but we have no shoes which are large inside and small outside."

Your president has recalled some of Mrs. Belmont's accomplishments and I must simply take his text and elaborate on it for a few minutes. It is not possible to record all the reasons why the National Institute of Social Sciences has been moved to confer its medal upon Mrs. August Belmont — Eleanor Robson Belmont. But the mere mention of her name brings to the minds of us all one of the reasons. In the early years of this century Eleanor Robson was one of the bright, particular stars of the American stage. Who that ever saw her can forget her as Merely Mary Ann, as Salomy Jane, as Juliet to Kyrle Bellew's Romeo? George Tyler, her old manager, speaks of "that strange pure charm" which she possessed, "very fragile and yet tremendously real." As for the rest of us we know that in both comedy and tragedy she showed enormous intelligence, sympathy and dramatic capacity. And in her voice alone — then as today — she had more alluring charm than ought to be vouchsafed to any one mortal!

And I cannot help but feel that with all her achievements of later years Eleanor Belmont never found life more thrilling than in those early days on the stage — that eager young girl of seventeen, with her hair still down her back, unknown, unlettered and unsung, journeying to San Francisco to make, almost tremulous perhaps, her first essay upon the stage. And you recall too, that no less a personage than George Bernard Shaw has never ceased complaint because Mrs. Belmont, Eleanor Robson as she was then, never acted in that play that he wrote especially for her. Mr. Shaw, like the entire public in London, was enthralled with Miss Robson's performance of *Merely Mary Ann,* and determined to write a play for her. He did write the play and called it *Major Barbara.* But fortune decreed that Eleanor Robson should never act it. As I say, George Bernard Shaw has never forgiven the fates and he complains to me about it to this very day.

Marriage took Eleanor Robson from the stage, but it only placed her in a wider plain of high endeavor.

> All the world's a stage,
> And all the men and women merely players.

The world became the stage upon which Eleanor Belmont came to play. In the crowded years before the Great War her aid was given to plans for helping promising young players for the American stage, to prison reform and to other beneficent movements which I cannot possibly catalogue. And then came the further blossoming of her talents in the days of American participation in the Great War. I like to think of her association in Red Cross leadership with my beloved partner, the late Henry Pomeroy Davison. Red Cross in the war rallied and led America to one of the fine things in its history — a magnificent outpouring of generosity and devotion. Mrs. Belmont became assistant to the Chairman of the Red Cross War Council, and was a central point of inspiration for all the women in the country in Red Cross. In Washington, in New York and up and down the land she labored night and day, working and speaking in those moving terms which only she could command.

Upon Mrs. Belmont's work throughout the depression one could write a volume. Year after year she was the head of the Women's Division which did such extraordinary work in raising those great sums through which the private citizens of New York showed their appreciation of the need at their doors and their determination to meet it. "No one shall go hungry or without shelter whom we can reach" was their slogan. And what counted perhaps fully as much as the money was the attitude which Mrs. Belmont and her fellow-workers assumed. This was not an objective piece of work which they were doing. No, this was something far more intimate and compelling. "Love thy neighbor as thyself" was exemplified in every word uttered, every action taken by Mrs. Belmont in those difficult days.

And in the organizations which she built up were shown her true qualities of character and leadership. What was it that gave her the power to get people to work with an unending devotion to her and to the cause? Her personality, of course, but even more her unselfishness, her infinite industry, her humor and sense of proportion. Above all, if she will let me say so, something spiritual in her makeup, that flame that brings the light of her heart into her face and eyes and whole radiant presence.

Mrs. Belmont, you are almost the only person I know who is a living refutation of that verse in the Bible which says "Woe unto you when all men shall speak well of you." This medal has been heretofore bestowed upon presidents of our country, upon statesmen and leaders of men. Never more worthily than tonight upon you!

William Lyon Phelps presents
Sir William Llewellyn

Portrait painter, president of the Royal Academy of Arts, London, and delegate to the proceedings of the American Academy of Arts and Letters, November 13, 1930, Sir William Llewellyn was introduced on this occasion by William Lyon Phelps of Yale University.

A GREAT many people say, of course, that the English have no humor, that is, I have heard that in America; but it really is not a lack of humor because they are the most humorous people in the world. They are the only people who can take jokes on their own country with delight. Their sense of humor extends to nationalism, but they don't understand jocosity from strangers on account of the climate. For example, on a very hot day in America when it is about ninety-six in the shade and you are walking along the street and meet another American, a stranger, he will say, "Don't you wish you had brought your overcoat?" and you reply and walk on. But if you meet an Englishman on the street on a day like that and say "Don't you wish you had brought your overcoat?" he would look at you in bewilderment and say, "Of course you mean your *light* overcoat." It doesn't prove he hasn't a sense of humor, it means he doesn't know why a perfect stranger should attempt to be funny with him.

I remember in Vancouver, British Columbia, once I sat down at dinner with an Englishman whom I hadn't seen before, and just in order to start something, I said:

"Of course in Vancouver you are away behind the times, but I don't see why you advertise the fact."

"What on earth do you mean?" he said.

"Look at your card," I said. "Vancouver, B.C."

"But it doesn't mean that, you know," he said.

There again it is not that they are deficient in humor. Why should a stranger attempt to treat him like a member of the family? Those who believe the English have no sense of humor are going to get into trouble.

I remember an incident of three Americans talking together who agreed that the English had no sense of humor. At that moment an Englishman approached them and the three agreed that he should then and there be put to the test. So one of the Americans stopped the Englishman and narrated a side-splitting yarn. The Englishman listened to it with a face of leather. The American said, "Buck up, old man, you will laugh at that next summer."

The Englishman said, "No, I think not."

"Why not?"

"I laughed at that *last* summer."

So you see they have a sense of humor, the only difference being that it is rather better than the American. At any rate it is best not to comment upon their not possessing it. Someone said, and I think this goes to the root of a national distinction, "The American humor consists in overstatement and English humor in understatement," and you see that is a real distinction.

I should like a better understanding of the geography of England by the Americans and to a less extent an understanding of American geography by Englishmen. I prepared once a literary map of England and I required all my students at Yale to learn that map so they would know what is meant when Tennyson speaks of Lincolnshire. I had a remarkable testimony from one of the undergraduates. He said, "Dear Mr. Phelps: I bicycled across England carrying your map. I placed it inside my shirt and I found it saved me from having pneumonia."

I was talking to an Englishman and he said, "You talk about our names. It is just as bad in America."

I said, "How is that?"

He said, "Look at one of your great western states. You spell it I-o-w-a and then you pronounce it Ohio."

You see we can turn these differences into a matter of concord by laughing at them, which is the best solution in the world of nearly all apparent discrepancies and difficulties. At any rate, whatever people say, whatever trivial disturbances may come, we know we are one flesh and one blood, and I present to you Sir William Llewellyn, President of the Royal Academy of Arts, London. We are delighted to have him with us today.

Howard S. Cullman presents
Roger L. Stevens

Real estate broker and producing partner in over one hundred Broadway plays, Roger Stevens was introduced by Howard S. Cullman, president of the Lotos Club, on the occasion of a state dinner in honor of Frederic March and Florence Eldridge.

ROGER STEVENS has led a triple life. First, as a prominent realtor, and while not an empire builder, he bought and sold the Empire State Building; second, he probably was the most prodigious producer on Broadway over a span of many years and imported practically every play that was successful in London; third, today as president of the National Council on the Arts, with offices in the White House, he is responsible for grants for music, ballet, the theatre, and art.

We as a young country have been derelict in subsidizing the arts. England has had its Fine Arts Council; France, the Comédie Française and the Opéra. Vienna heavily subsidizes its opera, and the same is true of Sweden, Norway, and Finland; and I believe even Moscow has over a span of years subsidized its theatre, ballet, and music. We are familiar with the royal Japanese productions as well, including the kabuki, financed by the Japanese government.

We are a little late in starting, but under Roger Stevens' dynamic leadership we are going to have a wonderful President Kennedy Memorial in Washington and substantial grants to the arts through the courtesy of the last Congress. It is a great privilege to introduce you to the dispenser, Roger Stevens.

George Jessel presents
Jack Benny

When many of his contemporaries are retiring, Jack Benny keeps on standing — with that look that causes warm and jovial laughter to ripple across the room. This introduction of Jack Benny appears in George Jessel's book entitled *You Too Can Make a Speech*, published by the Grayson Publishing Corporation in 1956. Mr. Jessel has been aptly described as the "Toastmaster General of the United States."

THE NEXT speaker I have known for over thirty years. I played in vaudeville with him thirty years ago, while playing in vaudeville with his partner, Mr. Woods, who was highly intelligent and handsome by comparison. He was also a traveling salesman and everybody loved him because he was coming through those towns for years and years. I am giving you this data on him so it isn't possible that he could only be thirty-nine — since I have seen people meet him at the stage door thirty years ago and say: "Gee, Jack, you must miss your old pal, William McKinley...."

I don't see as much of him as I used to — in fact, hardly anybody sees him but the Ronnie Colmans. They say he has one older brother who is kept in a trunk and only comes out for Passover. But, despite all of his idiosyncrasies and his supposed stinginess he is beloved not only throughout this nation, but, I might say, nearly all over the world.

Although he is known for his other vocations — and fortunately he has them — he has also been a producer. He produced one film — *The Lucky Stiff* — which, while it never played in any of the first-run theaters or the second- or third-run theaters, or even the drive-ins — was very often used in penitentiaries and comfort stations. However, he was an astute enough producer to sell this project along with some other planned disasters to the Columbia Broadcasting System for some two million dollars.

He was in one picture as an actor that was so bad that Arthur Hornblow sued him because his name was in the title. Even the new picture *Horatio Hornblower* — they may have to change to *Harry Hines.*

He is known and beloved from Waukegan to Wimpole Street — from Kishinev to Korea — from Pennsylvania to Polly Adler — Mr. Jack Benny.

George Jessel *presents*
Groucho Marx

This introduction of one of the famed Marx brothers appears in George Jessel's book entitled *You Too Can Make a Speech*, published by the Grayson Publishing Corporation in 1956.

THERE ARE many, many brothers who have gained fame — from the Maccabees of old Israel who conquered in Judea, the Wright Brothers who conquered the air, the Ritz Brothers who conquered gin rummy, down to the Marx Brothers. . . .

As you know, there's Gummo, who manages the next speaker. This certainly doesn't take a great deal of his time, as he is always here playing cards. . . . Zeppo, who has a large factory making metal parts which, by a strange coincidence, is next to the Sands Hotel in Las Vegas. . . . Chico, who is in the mining game. He has a mine where they have drilled for gold and after going down twelve levels, they found a deck of pinochle cards. . . . Then there is another brother, Louso, who disappeared altogether in Canada with some samples he had taken from a bank. . . . And there's Harpo, who refuses to make any comment. . . . And last, the noblest Marx of them all, who has heckled himself into millions of dollars — Groucho Marx. . . .

THE LITERARY

WORLD

Lionel Trilling presents

T. S. Eliot

On April 28, 1958, T. S. Eliot gave a poetry reading to an enthusiastic audience at Columbia University. He was introduced by Lionel Trilling, professor of English at Columbia, well known for his studies of Matthew Arnold and E. M. Forster, as well as other critical writings.

MR. BARZUN has suggested how absurd it would be to think of introducing Mr. Eliot to this audience, or to any audience. And indeed what is really needed on an occasion like this is some way of de-introducing Mr. Eliot — I wish there were some formula that I might utter that would for a while remove from our minds all our intense awareness of Mr. Eliot's achievement, all recollection of our agreement or disagreement with his doctrinal positions in criticism or religion or politics, all memory of the lectures about his work we have given or heard and of the essays about him we have written or read. I should like to see us for a little time wrapped in a cloud of unknowing, such as used to envelop us, or some of us, a good many years ago.

Somewhere in my university office is a copy of *The Dial* for November 1922, in which *The Waste Land* first appeared in this country. I can remember how I read it — with some resentment, in a fever of incomprehension, having only the sense that it was important and very moving, that it was about my own life and the unhappy epoch that I, as a Columbia College sophomore, was condemned to live in. There were no notes of any kind, not even Mr. Eliot's, although these were promised. I knew enough Latin to understand that the Sybil in the epigraph was in a bad situation, but no Greek to know what question the boys put to the Sybil, nor what she answered them. It did not very much matter — it did not matter that I could not understand the poem. After a little while there came to the help of my incomprehension the theory which then prevailed that the poem was to be understood as music is understood, that the best way to perceive what was going on in the poem was to read it aloud, and that it did not matter if one failed to understand in a precise way this allusion or that. It was a simple theory and an inadequate one, but it was essentially correct. Whoever first reads the poem, or any of Mr. Eliot's poems, according to that prescription cannot go far wrong. But the inadequacies of the simple theory had to be supplied, and they were supplied, and now *The Waste Land* has been glossed and annotated by a hundred busy and competent hands. Not an allusion but has been tracked down and securely nailed to the floor. And the same devoted effort has been directed upon all of Mr. Eliot's poems — can we doubt that on some American campus at this very moment some graduate student is preparing a theoretical basis for our understanding of the *Practical Cats?*

That the work of explication needed to be done there can be no doubt. Yet as Mr. Eliot himself has become increasingly aware, the explicatory impulse began to stand in the way of his poems. And over recent years, in one way or another, he has in effect said what Wordsworth once said: "Must eyes be all in all, the tongue and ear Nothing?" It might of course be objected that his protest against being understood only through ideas and images is a compromised one — if he had wanted to be understood immediately and emotionally he should not have written difficult poetry. Yet whoever has responded to Mr. Eliot's poetry knows that sound plays as great a part in it as ideas and images, that there really is to be heard in it the most subtle of all musics, the music of thought and the music of feeling, that Mr. Eliot is telling the literal truth about the nature of the poetic process when in his essay "The Music of Poetry" he says, "I know that a poem, or a passage of a poem, may tend to realize itself first as a particular rhythm before it reaches expression in words, and that this rhythm may bring to birth the idea and the image."

Mr. Eliot is said to have said that for his poetry he would prefer an illiterate audience. It is not for me to say whether or not we have provided him with what he wants. I leave it to each one of you to show Mr. Eliot the hospitality you would wish to show him by making yourself for this evening if not illiterate — that is perhaps beyond your powers — then at least as simple and direct in your response to what you hear as he would desire.

James L. Godfrey presents
Frank Borden Hanes

Frank Borden Hanes, North Carolina novelist and poet, spoke on the subject "Theme Sources of Three Novels" at the 1961 annual meeting of the Friends of the Library of the University of North Carolina. He was introduced by James L. Godfrey, Distinguished University Professor of History of the University of North Carolina.

MAY I make some expression for myself and for all of us of our gratitude for this occasion and our pleasure in being here. This is by all odds one of the significant meetings of the academic year, for we have come together in recognition of the importance of books and the library to the University and to the world of learning. This brings us very near to the heart of the University's real reason for existence and enables us to pay some personal respect to the sphere of letters and the accumulated record that marks so much of human creativity. This morning with the welcome, though awesome, news of the successful flight of Commander Shepard, we paid our deep respects to courage and skill; this evening we can round out the day by the tribute we pay here to the symbols of wisdom and understanding. We shall need all of these as we make our way.

We are to have the pleasure of hearing a most versatile young man. I say young, for so he seems to me with a youthfulness of spirit as well as age, and I describe him as versatile since he has such a wide and successful interest in a number of things. He is an industrialist — not a tycoon perhaps — but nonetheless a director of a considerable enterprise. He is a public-spirited citizen who gives time and attention to cultural and civic affairs and has long been on the barricades in the struggle for better opportunities for education. He turns his hand to philanthropy when the cause is sufficiently tempting, and many of us will recall him warmly for his gracious presentation of the millionth volume to the University Library last October. He also is eminently successful as a family man with a charming wife and three children. These qualities are great enough and varied enough to recommend him to us, but the one that appeals to us most this evening is that he is a man of letters, a novelist and poet, the author of two published novels, with a third on the way.

One must marvel at the self-discipline that finds time in such a busy life for literary work. Where there is so much that is good, this is an extra bit — a sort of overplus — that leads us to admire all the more so many solid virtues augmented by creative imagination and talent. That this author is also a Hanes — one of a family whose benefactions have had fruitful results for our Library — makes him doubly welcome here.

Lucile Nix presents

Edmon Low

The Librarian of Oklahoma State University was introduced to the librarians of the University Center of Georgia at the Center's annual dinner meeting on April 11, 1967, by Lucile Nix, Chief of the Public Library Service.

INASMUCH AS this is a gathering of librarians, I have chosen to review for you tonight a new book entitled *Low Man High on the Totem Pole.* This is a publication with thousands of authors, all of them friends and co-workers of their subject who without doubt is a well known, beloved, and distinguished professional librarian, teacher, library buildings consultant, and scholar.

There is no evidence of bias present in the writing of the authors. This reviewer knows that this is true, since she has been associated with the subject and followed his career with admiration and respect over a period of years.

Mr. Low, or Mr. Oklahoma Librarian, as he is frequently called in the news in his state, has demonstrated superior leadership at every level of training and service in his chosen profession. The University of Illinois, where he received his B.S. in Library Science, and the University of Michigan, which granted him his master's in the field of librarianship, proudly claim him as an alumnus and one to whom high honors were awarded by both institutions.

In his career as a librarian the biographee has held important administrative positions in Ohio and in his native state of Oklahoma. Since 1940 he has served as Oklahoma State University Librarian and as its Dean since 1946.

Few people have been elected or appointed to more or higher offices or committee leadership roles than "good old Ed Low." Among these he has served as:

President, Oklahoma Library Association
President, Southwestern Library Association
Vice-President, American Library Association
President, Association of College and Research Libraries
Member, American Library Association Legislation Committee
Member, Shared Cataloging Committee of the Association of Research
    Libraries

Among the contributors to this biography is none other than Mr. Low's own secretary. She writes:

At the annual Oklahoma Library Association Conference held in March 1967, the whole program was devoted to honoring Mr. Low. Many national library leaders were here, and telegrams of appreciation were received from President Johnson, Vice-President Humphrey, Mr. Carl Albert, Senators Monroney and Harris, and Governor Bartlett. Representative Steed was the speaker at the conference banquet at which many state representatives were present. Our local paper ended a very laudatory editorial by saying, "And what about Low, the man?" This is probably best expressed by one of his staff members who said, "He always praises us for work well done, and covers up our mistakes."

This loyal and devoted secretary says further, "And my dentist said to me recently, 'They can get someone else in his place (when he retires) but they can't fill his shoes.'"

Is it any wonder that this book is called *Low Man High on the Totem Pole?* The authors speak frankly, factually, honestly, and from the heart. They could not do otherwise to their subject as you can now observe for yourself.

Mr. Edmon Low, Librarian and Dean of Oklahoma State University, and "Low Man High on the Totem Pole."

Martha A. Shull presents
Bruce Catton

No virtuoso of Civil War history now operating has proved able to evoke this period in our history so vividly and dramatically as the historian Bruce Catton. He is presented to the ninety-fifth annual meeting of the National Education Association by its president, Martha A. Shull.

THE FABRIC of our life today is a seamless web, whose pattern has been designed and woven by the acts and by the thoughts and the beliefs of people whom we never knew. America is a very great country, both in material achievements and in its spiritual heritage. To understand the present and the possibilities of the future, it is necessary to look at the past — at the deeds and the ideas of men, and at the faith that has guided them.

Our speaker this afternoon is eminently qualified to speak on "The Spiritual Heritage of America." He is well known as a historian who has succeeded in portraying effectively not only the events of the past, but also the motives and ideals of the people who made the events. By helping us to understand them, he helps us to appreciate our heritage.

Mr. Catton is perhaps best known for his book *A Stillness at Appomattox*, for which he was awarded the Pulitzer Prize for historical literature in 1954. He has written many other books and is the editor of the remarkable publication known as the *American Heritage* series. He started his career as a reporter on the *Cleveland News* and has held other posts in newspaper work and in special service with the government. His interest is always in the human aspects of history and in the nature of man. This is shown by a sentence in a short article of his in *This Week* magazine, concerning the recent naval review at Hampton Roads: "Under everything else, the fate of nations and the progress of the race itself is built on the dedication and the valor of ordinary mortals who have found something larger than themselves to serve."

The spiritual heritage of America is certainly the foundation for all we think and all we do. It is very fortunate that Bruce Catton, a man of knowledge and of insight, is to start our convention by speaking on "The Spiritual Heritage of America." . . . Mr. Catton.

Oliver Wendell Holmes presents
Matthew Arnold

In the fall and winter of 1883–1884, Matthew Arnold, English poet, classical scholar, and literary critic, visited the United States to deliver his famous series of lectures, published as *Discourses in America*. The essayist, poet, and physician Oliver Wendell Holmes introduced him on the occasion of his appearance in Boston to deliver the first in his lecture series.

LADIES AND GENTLEMEN: The position in which I find myself this evening reminds me of a story told me by a schoolmate, a nephew of the late Washington Allston, in reference to Mr. Edmund Dana. He was of short stature, and was walking the streets of London with a gentleman much taller than himself, when the latter was run against by one of those persons styled roughs, but more fittingly ruffians. The gentleman who experienced the collision promptly handed his coat to the little man, and struck an attitude of resistance. The conference was not a long one, and the tall man having got the better of it, one of the English crowd, who always like fair play, shouted, "Hurrah for the gentleman." Another voice supplemented the cry with, "And hurrah for the little man that held his coat." The friend who was to have played the part of the "little man" of my story was Rev. Phillips Brooks, who is unfortunately prevented from coming this evening by indisposition. I have been asked to fill his place, which, in my point of view, is beyond my capacity. Happily, little is required of one who is to introduce the distinguished speaker of this evening. Were it only that he is the son of Thomas Arnold his welcome would be as wide as the realm over which the English language is spoken. Were he of unknown parentage he would be welcomed as a poet, the writer of noble verse, lofty and inspiring; as a critic, incisive, plain-spoken, honest, going to the heart of his subjects, the terror of Dagon and the Philistines; as a man worthy of the grand name he bears. I have the pleasure of introducing Mr. Matthew Arnold.

Richard T. Cragg presents
Cyril Northcote Parkinson

C. Northcote Parkinson, author and historian, first came to the attention of a wide popular audience following the appearance of an article in the London *Economist* in which he showed that as Britain's ships and colonies declined in number, the number of people needed for their administration increased. He produced a number of articles in similar vein which resulted in his book *Parkinson's Law* (1957). Speaking before the Executives' Club of Chicago, October 28, 1966, he was introduced by Richard T. Cragg, president of the Club.

ALMOST TEN YEARS AGO, administrators were chuckling at a joke on themselves. The source of their somewhat uneasy amusement was *Parkinson's Law*, a collection of essays that satirized managerial bureaucracy in business and government.

When the essays were first published anonymously in the London *Economist* in 1955, most of the readers thought that Professor C. Northcote Parkinson was just a creation of the jesting editors. Dr. Parkinson pointed out later, that "rumors of his nonexistence proved to be unfounded or at least grossly exaggerated."

When he first visited the United States in 1958, his book *Parkinson's Law* had already become a best seller, and he had come to be regarded as an authority on organizational efficiency.

Cyril Northcote Parkinson was born at Barnard Castle in the County of Durham, England. His early interests were painting and journalism. In fact, his lifelong interest in maritime and naval history stems from his early interest in painting ships and seascapes — an interest shared by his father.

In 1935 he received his Doctor of Philosophy degree at King's College, University of London. His dissertation was entitled *Trade and War in Eastern Seas, 1793–1813*. This dissertation was later expanded into other books. These in turn have been followed by other scholarly publications.

After teaching history in a series of academic posts, including the Royal Naval College in Dartmouth, until 1941, he joined the British Army where he served until demobilized in 1946. It was largely in the Army that Dr. Parkinson gained the firsthand experience that enabled him to formulate his first law, namely "work expands to fill the time available for its completion."

His exposé of the ludicrousness of much bureaucratic behavior has resulted in a double impact — it is read initially as a joke — but the sequel to laughter is the shock of realization that the statistics are accurate and that the wildest statement is literally true.

Although Dr. Parkinson has been subject to criticism for his forthright views on government and business, his down-to-earth realism and basic understanding of human reactions is universally respected. He is noted as a distinguished historian and educator — a vocation unrelated to the achievements for which he became so widely known. Expressing some surprise at the celebrity he has achieved, he states that it should be credited to sheer persistence.

The Executives' Club of Chicago has twice before had the pleasure of hearing Dr. Parkinson from our platform, so to many of you I reintroduce an old friend of the Club to tell us about "A Law Unto Themselves." Dr. C. Northcote Parkinson.

Sir Owen Seaman *presents*
Stephen Leacock

Stephen Leacock (1869–1944) was born in Hampshire, England, graduated from Upper Canada College, and received his doctorate from the University of Chicago. He is best known as a humorist, although as head of the Department of Political Science at McGill University, and as a lecturer and writer in the field of political economy, he was widely recognized in the scholarly world. On the occasion of his first lecture in London, he was introduced by Sir Owen Seaman, author, teacher, and editor of *Punch* (1906–1932). Many other introductions that he received on his lecture tours were not so felicitous. In his essay "We Have With Us To-night," from the collection *Laugh With Leacock* (1930), he recounts numerous instances of the tactlessness and unpreparedness of chairmen.

IT IS USUAL on these occasions for the chairman to begin something like this: "The lecturer, I am sure, needs no introduction from me." And indeed, when I have been the lecturer and somebody else has been the chairman, I have more than once suspected myself of being the better man of the two. Of course I hope I should always have the good manners — I am sure Mr. Leacock has — to disguise that suspicion. However, one has to go through these formalities, and I will therefore introduce the lecturer to you.

Ladies and Gentlemen, this is Mr. Stephen Leacock. Mr. Leacock, this is the flower of London intelligence — or perhaps I should say one of the flowers; the rest are coming to your other lectures.

In ordinary social life one stops at an introduction and does not proceed to personal details. But behavior on the platform, as on the stage, is seldom ordinary. I will therefore tell you a thing or two about Mr. Leacock. In the first place, by vocation he is a professor of political economy, and he practices humor — frenzied fiction instead of frenzied finance — by way of recreation. There he differs a good deal from me, who have to study the products of humor for my living, and by way of recreation read Mr. Leacock on political economy.

Further, Mr. Leacock is all-British, being English by birth and Canadian by residence. I mention this for two reasons: firstly, because England and the Empire are very proud to claim him for their own, and, secondly, because I do not wish his nationality to be confused with that of his neighbors on the other side. For English and American humorists have not always seen eye to eye. When we fail to appreciate their humor they say we are too dull and effete to understand it; and when they do not appreciate ours we say they haven't got any.

Now Mr. Leacock's humor is British by heredity; but he has caught something of the spirit of American humor by force of association. This puts him in a similar position to that in which I found myself once when I took the liberty of swimming across a rather large loch in Scotland. After climbing into the boat I was in the act of drying myself when I was accosted by the proprietor of the hotel adjacent to the shore. "You have no business to be bathing here," he shouted. "I'm not," I said; "I'm bathing on the other side." In the same way, if anyone on either side of the water is unintelligent enough to criticize Mr. Leacock's humor, he can always say it comes from the other side. But the truth is that his humor contains all that is best in the humor of both hemispheres.

Having fulfilled my duty as chairman, in that I have told you nothing that you did not know before — except, perhaps, my swimming feat, which never got into the Press because I have a very bad publicity agent — I will not detain you longer from what you are really wanting to get at; but ask Mr. Leacock to proceed at once with his lecture on "Frenzied Fiction."

John Adams Lowe presents
E. J. Pratt

On the occasion of the twenty-fifth anniversary of the Rochester Poetry Society, November 14, 1945, John Adams Lowe, Director of the Rochester Public Library (1932–1952), presented the distinguished Canadian poet E. J. Pratt as guest speaker.

THE SEA and seafaring fashioned the fabric of E. J. Pratt's thinking. Vast ice floes, gigantic whales, mighty ships, titans, illimitable space created for him an expansive mind and inclusive heart.

He grew up in a fishing village of Newfoundland, preached there and taught school. Victoria College of the University of Toronto made him a Master of Arts, a Doctor of Philosophy, and Professor of English Literature. Over bookstore counters have passed more than twenty thousand copies of his verse and heroic epics. His pen has earned for him the Royal Society Medal, "choicest of possessions," and two Governor-General's medals. *Brebeuf and His Brethren* was broadcast across the country on two occasions and Sir Ernest McMillan produced it with symphonic orchestra and chorus.

Canadians from coast to coast affectionately know him as "Ned" Pratt. Children learn his poems from their school readers. Critics place him eminently alongside Archibald Lampman and Duncan Campbell Scott as the ranking Canadian poet of this generation.

Therefore, for what he is, dynamic teacher, creator of friendliness and good will, distinguished poet, the Rochester Poetry Society celebrating its silver anniversary elects him to Honorary Membership and for the first time adds the name of a neighbor north of the border to its short but illustrious list. With such warm welcome, Ned, you shall never again be a stranger in Rochester.

Ladies and Gentlemen: Dr. Pratt.

George Bernard Shaw *presents*
Major Barbara

Here is an introduction spoken by George Bernard Shaw to the film version (released February 15, 1941) of his play *Major Barbara*. It is an unusual starring vehicle even for Shaw but one in which the spoken word, like most personal introductions, is not likely to be preserved in print. Therefore, because it is an introduction of sorts, because it is ephemeral, and because it is a characteristic Shaw piece, the compilers have included it in this anthology.

CITIZENS OF the United States of America, the whole 130 millions of you, I am sending you my old plays, just as you are sending us your old destroyers. Our Government has very kindly thrown in a few naval bases as well; it makes the bargain perhaps more welcome to you. Now, the German humorist, I think his name is Dr. Goebbels, he has got a great deal of innocent fun out of that. He tells us — or rather he tells the rest of the world — that England has sold her colonies for scrap iron. Well, why shouldn't we? We are in very great need of scrap iron. We are collecting iron from door to door. Our women are bringing out their old saucepans; our men are bringing out their old bicycles, and you, with equal devotion, are bringing out your old destroyers. Well, a very good bargain for us. Every one of those destroyers will be worth much more to us than their weight in bicycles and saucepans.

And now, what about our colonies? Our colonies are always much the better when we have plenty of Americans visiting them. You see, in America you have all the gold in the world. We have to barter things for want of that gold, and accordingly, when we see Americans coming along with gold to spend, when we think of our colonies with American garrisons in them, we are delighted.

If you had only known, we would have given you those naval bases — Dr. Goebbels calls them colonies, but let us be correct and call them naval bases — you could have had those naval bases for nothing but your friendship. Absolutely nothing. We should have been only too glad to have you. In fact, if you would like a few more, say in the Isle of Wight or the Isle of Man, or on the West Coast of Ireland, well, we shall be only too glad to welcome you. Delightedly!

Now, here I am in an English county, one of the counties that we call the home counties. I am within forty minutes' drive of the center of London, and at any moment a bomb may crash through this roof and blow me to atoms, because the German bombers are in the skies. Now, please understand, I can't absolutely promise you such a delightful finish to this news item. Still, it may happen, so don't give up hope — yet. If it does happen, well, it will not matter very much to me. As you see, I am in my eighty-fifth year. I have shot my bolt, I have done my work. War or no war, my number is up. But if my films are still being shown in America, my soul will go marching on, and that will satisfy me.

When I was a little boy, a child, just taught to read, I saw in the newspaper every day a column headed, "The Civil War in America." That is one of my first recollections. When I grew up they told me that that war in America had abolished black slavery, so that job having been done, I determined to devote my life as far as I could to the abolition of white slavery. That is just as much in your interest as it is in my interest or that of England. I hope you will have a hand in that abolition as you had a hand in the last abolition.

And I don't think I need detain you any longer. Look after my plays and look after my films. They are all devoted to the abolition of that sort of slavery. And I should like to imagine that when my mere bodily stuff is gone, I should like to imagine that you are still working with me, with my soul — in your old phrase — at that particular job. That is all I have to say. And so, farewell!

William Lyon Phelps presents
André Chevrillon

André Chevrillon, a scholar and member of the French Academy of Paris, was a delegate at the meeting of the American Academy of Arts and Letters, November 13, 1930. He was introduced by William Lyon Phelps of Yale University, president of the National Institute of Arts and Letters, and himself a man of letters of the largest reputation.

THE ONLY reason why I am chosen to speak before this gathering is because, as Shakespeare says, I am dressed in a little brief authority. For the moment I have the honor and the pleasure of being the President of the National Institute of Arts and Letters.

I thought this morning as we heard addresses in various languages that the whole progress of civilization might be illustrated by the change some six thousand years ago from the original international conference which was called the Tower of Babel to the present League of Nations. The Tower of Babel to the League of Nations illustrates the history of civilization, and you remember this morning, one of the speakers chose, with felicity and charm, to address us in the Latin language, what Browning called the language of marble, and then he turned to President Nicholas Murray Butler and addressed him not in the dialect of New York but in the dialect of Cicero. Then President Butler, who has never failed to be equal to a situation, responded in the same Latin tongue. That reminded me of the time when Yale University, which I serve, was holding its bicentennial in 1901. The delegates from various institutions in Europe and in America were presented to President Hadley and they addressed him for the most part in English. Just on my left stood a United States senator, who is now in heaven, or somewhere. In the line of delegates coming up to President Hadley was a large Swedish gentleman from Stockholm. Mr. Hadley expected that he would talk English, but he addressed him in a magnificent tirade of Latin. Hadley looked at him for a moment, and replied in the same tongue, even as Mr. Butler did this morning. Then the United States senator expressed his surprise. He said, "I didn't know Hadley could talk Swedish."

This is a National Institute of Arts and Letters. It is national, not nationalistic. Nationalism bears to patriotism the same relation that prejudice bears to principle, that superstition bears to religion. Nothing is more symptomatic of a narrow, provincial, and even vulgar mind than the nationalistic idea. Perhaps the highest form that the League of Nations can take is a league such as that gathered here today, a league of art, because beauty speaks the language of no one nation. We all appreciate paintings, statues, and architecture with our eyes, and we all love the universal language of music with our ears. Men and women who are interested in art and culture know that art and culture have no boundary lines. There is no geography, there is no flag in the creative mind. For example, in the year 1932, only two years away, the whole world will celebrate the one hundredth anniversary of Goethe, a German, and the last of the great poets of the world.

So today all who are interested in the language of the mind, all who are interested in the aspirations of the heart are gathered together to do honor to a true ideal of the human race.

I have the great pleasure, first of all, of presenting to you a member of the French Academy. Not only is he an intimate friend of many English scholars and English-speaking people but he is himself a nephew of Taine, and he has brought to us today from the French Academy a large collection of valuable books and articles which the French Academy gives to the American Academy.

Ladies and Gentlemen, I have the honor of presenting M. André Chevrillon.

Robert Lusty presents Sir Norman Birkett

At the eighth National Book League annual lecture held in London October 25, 1950, Lord Justice Birkett (1883–1962), an eminent lawyer and great bookman, delivered the address and was introduced by Robert Lusty, chairman of the National Book League.

IT IS FIRST my very great pleasure, as your Chairman, to introduce our new President, Sir Norman Birkett. Sir Norman was elected a year ago to succeed our beloved John Masefield on his retirement through ill health. Illness, unfortunately, prevented Sir Norman Birkett's presence at our annual meeting a year ago, and tonight is, therefore, the first opportunity of meeting publicly members of the National Book League.

By his acceptance of the presidency, Sir Norman has done great honor to the league. It was pointed out to him as something of an inducement that the position was really more honorary than onerous, a phrase which Mr. Churchill might describe as a "terminological inexactitude." In fact, Sir Norman has, in a great variety of ways, accomplished most invaluable work for the league. He is going to talk to us tonight on "The Use and Abuse of Reading." My talk, I feel, should be entitled "The Use and Abuse of Presidents," for we have never hesitated to call upon our President when we have required his great authority, and he has never hesitated to comply with every request we have made.

Secondly, it is my privilege to offer to Sir Norman the warm congratulations of every member of the league on his recent elevation to the great position of Lord Justice.

Thirdly, and finally, I want to say how deeply grateful we are to him for accepting, during his first year of presidency, our invitation to deliver the Annual Lecture. By doing this, he is establishing a precedent which we hope will always be followed in the years to come.

I now have the very greatest pleasure in asking Sir Norman Birkett to deliver the Eighth Annual Lecture of the National Book League.

Guy Stanton Ford *presents*

Christopher Morley

Christopher Morley (1890–1957), American journalist and essayist, was introduced on the occasion of the fiftieth anniversary celebration of the Minneapolis Public Library by the former President of the University of Minnesota. Morley's favorite introduction was one he gave on the occasion of a booksellers' dinner where Will Durant, then in his first fanfare, was the guest. It so happened Morley had heard Dr. Durant's speech two or three times before. So he rose and said: "Gentlemen, Will Durant is the easiest of all speakers to introduce. All I have to say (and here he beamed lovingly upon him) is, Will, Do Rant — and he does!"

OUR GUEST speaker tonight is a most happy choice. It is a great privilege to have him here and to welcome him, because few writers of any kind have so distilled into their own writings the best of books, and no writer that I read from time to time more often makes me wish that I could lay aside other things and go and read some of the books that he pricks me on to with renewed interest. Could anyone be more appropriate as a speaker in behalf and on the occasion of the fiftieth anniversary of the Library than one who has enriched literature himself, and has recalled it to the living memories of all those who have followed his happy suggestions and been inspired by his own broad reading and scholarship?

It is a great pleasure to introduce Mr. Christopher Morley, writer, journalist, and scholar.

Chester R. Davis *presents*
Will Durant

Dr. Durant, author, philosopher, and lecturer, is perhaps best known for his popular book *The Story of Philosophy* (1926). Since Chester Davis made his introduction of Dr. Durant before the Executives' Club of Chicago, the last four volumes of his monumental series, *The Story of Civilization*, have appeared.

WE ARE living in a troubled world, beset with conflicts and confusion. We are all seeking enlightened leadership and reassurance. Even psychiatrists, when meeting today, attempt to reassure each other with the greeting, "You're all right, how am I?"

It is difficult for us to look at our problems objectively, and analyze world conditions philosophically. We welcome any clear thinking individual who can show us that *Faith* is justified by *Reason*.

Such a man, whom we are privileged to hear for the tenth time today, is Dr. Will Durant.

He, more than anyone else in our generation, has shown us history and philosophy are the living subjects that they are.

He is a Massachusetts product of French Canadian descent; educated in parochial schools, St. Peter's College in New Jersey, and Columbia University from which he received his degree of Doctor of Philosophy in 1917.

He has taught history, languages, and philosophy at Seton Hall College in New Jersey and Columbia University. He has lectured in the Presbyterian Church in New York on philosophy, history, biology, and economics. He has traveled twice around the world and four times through Europe in gathering material for his books with which most of you are familiar.

His first book, published in 1926, entitled *The Story of Philosophy*, holds a lasting place in American literature. Here was philosophy shorn of scholasticism and welcomed to over two million American homes. Yet oddly enough, this book was actually a by-product of Dr. Durant's major interest in life. Thirty-seven years ago he conceived the plan for a comprehensive story of civilization. In the course of research on this project, a sincere student with limited funds, he wrote *The Story of Philosophy*. The proceeds from that enabled him to devote all of his attention to his major project, and so far he has written four books dealing with the different phases of the comprehensive story of civilization.

Two more are scheduled for publication: *The Renaissance and the Reformation* for 1955 and *The Age of Reason* for 1960. Dr. Durant told me today that he hoped to speed that up a little bit, but that isn't because he has lost his faith in civilization. I am sure that most of you have read his books and are familiar with the witty, almost Gaelic style with which Dr. Durant enlivens his pages. He is equally interesting, thought-provoking, and entertaining as a speaker.

Before he knew this was to be Ladies' Day, he had chosen for his subject, "Our Morals — A Forthright Speech for Men." I have asked him to speak out and not to leave anything from his talk. I know you will be interested in hearing him. It is my pleasure to introduce Dr. Durant.

BUSINESS

James E. Day presents
John L. Lewis

As everyone knows, it was John L. Lewis's indomitableness in the face of the mighty that made him the ideal president of the United Mine Workers of America (1920–1960) during its struggles with the operators, Congress, the White House, the courts, and an outraged public opinion. He is introduced to a meeting of the Executives' Club of Chicago by James E. Day, president of the Midwest Stock Exchange.

FOR AN indeterminable number of years we have worked long and patiently to sign up our speaker of today. It is then with pardonable pride that I have the privilege to introduce him.

Now, it is a matter of record that the Empire State Building sways over three feet in a strong wind. In the lifetime of our speaker, in the most violent winds of controversy, there has never been a perceptible movement. To withstand such winds that at times have reached almost hurricane force would require a sound and solid base.

After interviewing both friend and foe, you soon discover the qualities that give our speaker his unwavering stability. His friends point admiringly to his fortitude and integrity; his enemies invariably, but grudgingly, admit that there never was a question about his courage and honesty.

Yes, our speaker has his share of enemies, but he has more than an ample quota of real friends. A number of them are the heads of our largest coal companies, with whom he has had many a rough battle.

I happen to come from a coal-mining town downstate. As a boy, I knew many men who worked in the deep mines, never seeing the sun. I can tell you that these men hold "John L.," as they call him, in high regard and with deep affection.

One of my interviews was with the chairman of the board of one of our outstanding coal companies headquartered here in Chicago. In reminiscing about Mr. Lewis, he said, "You know, John would have made a great general. Whenever he went into battle for his union, he always had several plans of attack. He could switch from one to another, as the circumstances warranted. I guess that's one of the reasons he generally won. I could almost say 'Ouch' right now when I think of some of the hard bargains he struck with me."

Gentlemen, the Executives' Club of Chicago is proud to present American Labor's five-star general, Mr. John L. Lewis.

Donald J. Erickson presents
W. E. Whitehead

Commander Whitehead, president of Schweppes (U.S.A.), Ltd., and the man whose bearded face in Schweppes advertisements is familiar to thousands, was introduced to the Executives' Club of Chicago by its president, Donald J. Erickson.

GOOD AFTERNOON, Ladies and Gentlemen. Although our guest's beard plays a subordinate role to his true function as American President, Canadian Chairman, Overseas Director, and Board Member of Schweppes, Ltd., to Americans it is synonymous with Commander Whitehead — the man from Schweppes. However, what most of his public will never know is that it was grown to save a mustache.

At the start of World War II, when our guest appeared before his selection board, he was told that if he joined the navy he would have to give up his magnificent mustache, to which he replied, "If that is all I shall lose, I'll have little cause for complaint."

However, pride of ownership prevailed and since, in the Royal Navy, a "full set" is acceptable, the mustache was saved. But when the Commander joined Schweppes in 1950, Sir Frederic Hooper, the head of the company, thought that it was time for this war relic to go. As Mrs. Whitehead tells the story in her delightful book, "Teddy hadn't thought of disagreeing until his two women wept over him."

When Sir Frederic came to persuade them otherwise, their determination completely undermined him, and, as usual, the ladies got their way. Later Sir Frederic admitted that they had done Schweppes a great service.

As Commander Whitehead's responsibilities grew, he was developing the overseas empire for Schweppes. Since the 1790's the company hadn't trusted any bottle abroad until it had been sealed in

63

one of their own plants. Under this system, the product traveled "laboriously and expensively from England by train, ship, sampan, raft, canoe, llama, mule, and, on safari, balanced on the heads of sweating bearers." This raised the price to as much as a pound in the Middle East and sixty cents per bottle in the United States.

After successful experiments with local bottling, the Commander came to the United States to make arrangements to have Schweppes bottled here, using local water treated to their standards, with the elixir imported from England. This step reduced the cost to sixteen cents.

To introduce the product to Americans, Commander Whitehead was prevailed upon by David Ogilvy to appear in the advertising campaign. Against his will, he posed, "just this once," alighting from a BOAC plane carrying the secrets of Schweppes. Response was so good that, as we know, the Commander has had to continue his starring role.

Whitehead the man rides, sails, fox-hunts, beagles, and walks forty blocks to his office every morning he is in town. Since his arrival in the United States, he has been an untiring advocate of Britain and British exports. He is presently chairman of the British Exports Marketing Advisory Committee, and last month accompanied Prince Philip on his tour. He was in this very room, as a matter of fact.

Ladies and Gentlemen, it is with great anticipation that I give you the Commander to tell us what it is like to be a status symbol. Commander Whitehead.

Louis Nizer presents
Grover A. Whalen

Grover A. Whalen, president of the New York World's Fair, 1939, and official "welcomer" of distinguished visitors to New York, is introduced here by Louis Nizer, prominent New York lawyer, whose fascinating book of courtroom stories and tactics, My Life in Court, was published in 1961.

WHAT ZIEGFELD did for the American girl, what Whiteman did for jazz, what Cecil B. DeMille did for the bathtub, what Vallee did for crooning — that's what Grover Whalen did for the New York police and the World's Fair. In other words, he glorified them.

It is a little difficult to welcome a champion welcomer. Do you remember those hot summer days when Grover Whalen rode up the canyons of Broadway in a snowstorm of ticker tape? The gardenia he wears today seems to me to represent that ticker tape concentrated into one little spot in his lapel.

In your younger days, gentlemen, you probably read Horatio Alger's stories. Well, instead of telling you the story I will tell you the title: "The World's Fair." Need I comment on the title of the new melodrama our hero enacts today at Flushing Meadows?

I said that Mr. Whalen glorified the police.

That was his most important contribution. We still have his traffic system, his police college, his airplane squad but, above all, he heroized the law instead of crime and that is the important psychological approach to the crime problem. He debunked the criminal. He built a wall of scorn around him — if you permit me to say so, the "Whalen" Wall at which criminals whined and sobbed.

Today he has the unique position of American ambassador-at-large on American soil to most of the nations of the world. His achievement lies in the fact that he has persuaded the governments to visit him as ambassador, construct their buildings, and join in the celebration of tomorrow's world.

In military life we have the Unknown Soldier who represents all the known soldiers. In civil life we ought to have a known citizen who represents all the unknown citizens.

I nominate for the office of known citizen of New York — Grover Whalen!

Clare E. Griffin presents

James Palmer

James Palmer, vice president and comptroller of Marshall Field and Company, spoke at the twenty-third annual meeting of the American Association of Collegiate Schools of Business, May 1, 1941. He was introduced by Clare E. Griffin, professor of business economics at the University of Michigan. The meeting was held at Minneapolis and the host on this occasion, Dean R. A. Stevenson of the University of Minnesota, had just given a Chamber of Commerce talk, in a scholarly sort of way, on the attractions of Minneapolis.

BEFORE STARTING on my part of the program, I merely want to remark as in Russell Stevenson's description of this territory, that in view of all the different ways in which one can leave this territory, either by way of the north; or by way of the east, and the St. Lawrence; and the south; it is a compliment to the territory that they have any people left up here.

The subject this evening, as Dean Jackson just said, is that of business research. We have all been interested in talking a great deal about the products of business research, and some trying to do a bit of business research, but I do not recall in a number of years, at any rate, that we have devoted a session of the annual meeting to the subject of business research; to talk *about* research rather than to present simply the products of research. I am glad to see business research given such an important position. Sometimes I think that we take our research too seriously. Research after all is, I assume, an orderly way of trying to arrive at facts; whether one does arrive at more reliable facts, and come nearer to the truth by those organized devices may remain a problem and perhaps some of the speakers will touch upon that during the course of the evening.

You will recall that there are various ways of estimating the weight of a pig. One is to look at the pig and make a guess of it; and another one which is consistent with the scientific method was suggested in this manner: One should get a plank, an oak plank of precise length, sixteen feet; balance that across a sharp edge until it is perfectly balanced; put your pig on one end of the plank, and then on the other end of the plank you pile rocks; and when the plank comes up to a perfectly horizontal position so that by measurement it is shown to be perfectly horizontal, you estimate the weight of the rocks, and you know how heavy the pig is.

Such research is the scientific method of arriving at the weight of a pig and in a truly academic tradition I would be the last one to say it was not a most accurate way of doing it. Some people outside of our own circle might doubt that.

In arranging this program, one of the subjects that seemed to me to be very profitable to discuss would be that of the relation between business research and business policy. We all pretend to be teaching business policy and so we are all teaching methods of business research, and there are some very serious questions in my mind of just what the relationship is, just how far business research can contribute to business policy. Having that question in my mind for some time and having the opportunity to make the program, I decided I was going to include that topic; when I began to cast about to get the man in the country who I thought was best fitted to talk on it, my thought turned to my friend Jim Palmer. One reason for that decision is that Palmer has been in academic work, as you know. He was a graduate student at the University of Chicago, and later a member of the faculty for fifteen years. He was a business consultant during that time so he was combining his academic work and practical application and now he has left the University of Chicago to work with Marshall Field and Company where he is vice president and comptroller. He has kindly consented to come up here, even though it meant coming at the last minute and leaving shortly after the meeting to get back to his duties; and I want to tell him now that I appreciate a great deal his courtesy in coming. He will speak to you on the subject "Relation of Business Research to Business Policy."

Job E. Hedges presents
Edward D. Duffield

Edward D. Duffield (1871–1938) was president of the Prudential Insurance Company of America, a lawyer, and for one year (1932–1933) acting president of Princeton University, of which he was a life trustee. He was introduced at the seventeenth annual meeting of the Association of Life Insurance Presidents, December 6, 1923, by Job E. Hedges, attorney for the Association.

I HAVE AN unusually difficult and yet sadly happy function to perform this particular morning. I am to present to you the Chairman of this convention, an old time-worn friend of mine, who has outstripped me in the passage of time, and is now older than I am.

Some years ago, just six years after I was graduated, he entered Princeton. While I was a senior, he, as a youthful resident of that university town, was always in my way, playing tennis around the campus, playing it very indifferently, as he plays golf, and yet I learned to have a very affectionate regard for him. In the process of time, he has gone on and on, and sentimentally, to my great distress, has become president of a great company.

The problem with me is whether the evolution from a human being into the presidency of a great corporation will destroy all those charming human instincts which have created the friendship between us which I have enjoyed — and I fear for him. I am not certain but what, while I introduce him, I must bid him farewell.

The demands of executive authority are so permeating, persistent, and all-powerful that many a good, wholesome, normal man has been ruined as such by being made president of a great company, as he has no one to associate with then. The necessary process of concentration, authority, and continuous elevation keeps putting him to a higher and higher point, until he has no associates at all, and that

69

is the demand, the inexorable demand of business. So, while I present officially a man who years ago was much younger than I was, he has now proceeded in point of responsibility until he looks down upon me from the altitude of age, and certainly from responsible authority.

I present him to you, but I bid him good-bye. Never after today will I feel sure that he feels the same toward me as I used to feel that he felt.

I have got that off my mind. I have performed the contractual requirements of my duties, and I present to you for your presiding officer, the Honorable Edward D. Duffield, President of the Prudential Insurance Company of America, and I bid a last fond farewell to my former personal intimate and soul-satisfying friend.

Thomas S. Lamont presents
Paul G. Hoffman

At the November 10, 1949, meeting of the Academy of Political Science, Paul Hoffman, then chairman of the board of directors of the Fund for the Republic, was speaking in his capacity as administrator of the Economic Cooperation Administration of the European Recovery Program. He was introduced on this occasion by Thomas S. Lamont (son of Thomas W. Lamont), vice president of J. P. Morgan and Company and a trustee of the Academy.

PAUL HOFFMAN came up the hard way — to the leadership of the Studebaker Corporation — and he proved that a company does not have to be gigantic to compete successfully with giants. He ran a very good show there, and it still runs well even though he is absent, which I think speaks well for his ability in picking men. And on that subject of picking men, I want to read a letter I had from a friend. He writes:

I had a chance to see ECA's operations in many countries this summer. Some businessman has said that it has too many bureaucrats, but if they themselves had recruited its personnel, they would have ended up with no better or more capable staff than Paul Hoffman's. Planning has been well done and controls seem reasonable and workable. Our ECA is well operated.

I value that opinion especially because it comes not from one of us soft-headed international do-gooders of Wall Street, as some of our Chicago friends occasionally call us, but from a hard-boiled, hard-headed Chicago industrialist who practically every morning of his life glues his eyes to the *Chicago Tribune*.

It was during the early years of the war that Paul Hoffman first became a national figure. He had a shrewd worry that American businessmen, in their great war effort, might overlook the difficulties

71

which would confront us all when the war ended. He felt it only prudent to prepare for postwar reconversion. So the Committee for Economic Development was started. Mr. Hoffman knocked on the doors of a thousand corporations, even the bankers, soliciting their support in funds and in the loan of good men; and he borrowed good men also from our universities — many of them here tonight — who brought their fine talents to bear upon the reconversion problems. Businessmen and economists work together; businessmen learn from the economists, and I hope even occasionally vice versa! Their joint efforts exerted a powerful influence on the policies of our government and helped to bring about the successful transition of our country from war to peace.

As I looked through some old clippings about Paul Hoffman, I ran across one unusual discrepancy. *Business Week* said he played golf in the high nineties, whereas *Life* said that he shot his golf in the low eighties, that that was his normal score. This indication that Paul Hoffman boasted to one of Harry Luce's reporters is the only evidence I have found of immodesty in this extraordinarily modest man.

Mr. Hoffman has just returned from Europe where he has been wrestling with a host of problems, and talking, in his usual candid fashion, with the foreign and finance ministers of the ECA-participating nations. Those men know, as we know, that once again Paul Hoffman has done a magnificent organizational job, that he has administered the largest, most difficult, most complicated selling and distribution operation in the history of the world, all with superlative skill throughout, with selfless energy and a disinterested nobility of motives that makes all of us very proud of him as an American. Mr. Paul Hoffman!

Henry Ford II *presents*
Elmo Roper

Speaking before the Economic Club of Detroit, December 6, 1950, Elmo Roper, marketing consultant and at that time research director, *Fortune* Survey of Public Opinion, was introduced by the presiding officer, Henry Ford II.

MR. CROW, Members of the Economic Club of Detroit, Ladies and Gentlemen: You may remember when General Stilwell walked out of Burma after the disastrous 1942 campaign he remarked simply, "We took a helluva beating."

And you may remember that when Jack Sharkey was knocked out by Jack Dempsey in 1927, he explained his defeat in four simple words, "I forgot to duck."

And you will probably also remember the famous statement by Mike Jacobs who attended a ball game in a snowstorm and declared afterwards, "I shoulda stood in bed."

Maybe at this point I should simply say, "Ladies and Gentlemen, I present Elmo Roper."

I couldn't be quite that cruel. As a matter of fact, I would like to take this opportunity to say a few words in defense of my friend Elmo Roper and of opinion research generally.

We have used his organization extensively to find out what people think about our products, and especially what our employees think about various problems and ideas important to management. We have a great respect for his integrity and his organization. And I remind you that he has been spectacularly right in the past, although he "took a helluva beating," "forgot to duck," and "shoulda stood in bed" in 1948.

As a matter of fact, Elmo Roper first attracted wide public attention by courageously sticking out his neck in 1936 and coming within

73

a statistical gnat's eyelash of hitting the popular vote on the button. And Elmo Roper, like General Stilwell, Jack Sharkey, and Mike Jacobs, had a simple, easily understood comment to make on November 4 regarding his election forecasts: "I was wrong," he said. "I don't know why, but I certainly propose to find out."

To help him find out he now has a distinguished committee of experts in the fields of mathematics, the social sciences, economics, psychology, political science, and business research. These experts have been drawn from Princeton, the University of Chicago, Williams, Harvard, Johns Hopkins, Yale, and the Columbia Broadcasting System.

I hope Elmo and his Social Science Research Committee find the answer they are looking for, and I feel sure that they will. I think there never was a time when it was more important for all of us to know and understand the viewpoint and opinions of large groups of people. Not simply customers and prospective customers; but employees, people in our plant towns, independent voters, large and small businessmen, and perhaps especially people in government. I don't mean that we need to know these things in order to cater to every whim of every group. That doesn't seem to me to be the objective of opinion research. I do mean we need to know in order to move constructively and effectively in the important world of people's ideas and opinions. It is just good intelligence work.

We on our part in the Ford Motor Company intend to use opinion research to the best possible advantage while people like Elmo and others find better techniques for getting more dependable answers. The sooner they do so, the better it will be for all of us. Meanwhile, we don't undervalue in any way, shape, or form the methods currently available.

And, now, I will say it is a great pleasure for me to present to you Elmo Roper.

Mr. Roper.

EDUCATION

Robert J. Blakely presents
Stephen Hayes Bush

Robert Blakely, editorial writer for the *Des Moines Register and Tribune*, introduced Professor Bush to a University of Iowa audience in April 1948 on the occasion of his approaching retirement. An expanded version of his remarks appears in the Iowa *Alumni Review*, April 1948.

I GIVE YOU a dangerous man, Stephen Hayes Bush, who since 1901 has been trying to teach his pupils to think.

But this is only a part of his heresy, for thinking is only a part of living, and few persons are really alive. The full charge against Stephen Bush is that for nearly fifty years he has been engaged in a ceaseless, robust, skillful attempt to do three seditious things: first, to teach pupils who are not really alive how to come alive; second, to teach pupils who are alive how to think; and, third, to teach pupils who can think how to live. He has unscrupulously used that most explosive of all teaching techniques — example.

A son of an old mercantile family in New England who went to the Boston Latin School and Harvard — why should he identify his entire working life with a relatively young and raw midwestern university? Bred and trained in the staid Anglo-Saxon culture of late nineteenth century New England — why should he have a life-long love affair with the Romance, and particularly the French, civilization? Why should a man nearly forty years old, who had been head of a department in a university for over ten years, take a leave of absence to serve with the French Foreign Legion in World War I? Why should a professor take up mountain climbing at the age of fifty-eight? Why should a man of sixty-five try to take part in the North African campaign of 1943?

The answer is really quite simple. Since boyhood Stephen Bush has fled, not from life, but from death and decadence, to life. He has always felt that if a man loses his life in an attempt to live it well, the price is little enough and well paid.

A man in high place at the University of Iowa once said, "Yes, Bush is a great teacher, but he has always lacked ambition. He has never tried to advance himself professionally." This touches the heart of the matter. Who should set a person's ambition — society or himself? Bush's ambition was to teach. Probably no other person in the history of the University of Iowa has had such a deep influence upon so many pupils as Stephen Bush.

Should a university try to educate the "natural aristocracy" or the "normal run"? The answer to this old debate is that it must do both. Some learned "educators" have written books proving conclusively that it can't do both. While they were writing their books, Stephen Bush has been doing both. He does both the only way both can be done — by giving himself completely to living minds. How do you recognize a living mind? Bush is not content with tests. He tries to breathe life into the nostrils of all who come his way. If he has to shock a reflex into a mind that is being delivered, Bush is good at holding a person by the heels and spanking his behind.

Stephen Bush is ageless. If there are any who do not find him contemporary, they are those of his own chronological age. For years, when head of the department of Romance languages, Bush insisted on teaching a freshman class so he could be acquainted with the new human material coming into the university. And his interest in his pupils never dies so long as their humanness has not died. Hundreds, perhaps thousands, of his former pupils treasure in their files letters which Bush wrote them in their hours of crisis — long, badly typed, single-spaced messages with their narrow margins flooded by footnotes in a curious backhanded scrawl, sharing grief over the death of a child, clarifying confusion over a divorce, easing disappointment in failure or shame in disgrace.

Stephen Bush is not beloved by all who know him. He is disliked by some and feared by many more. He is a good hater, a magnificent fighter and a scathing critic. He is a perennial "troublemaker" and he strives to inspire other "troublemakers." This is partly because he loves trouble for its own sake, but mainly it is because he wants to promote creative dissatisfaction.

Stephen Bush is all these things and many more. That is why he is a dangerous man — dangerous to all who are petty, self-satisfied, stupid, corrupt, pretentious, dishonest or cowardly.

I give you — if you can take him — this dangerous man, Stephen Hayes Bush.

Rose Z. Sellers presents
Harry D. Gideonse

The New York Library Club celebrated its seventieth anniversary in March 1955 with a dinner in honor of Dr. Harry D. Gideonse, President of Brooklyn College and chairman of the board of directors of Freedom House. Mrs. Rose Z. Sellers, associate librarian of Brooklyn College, introduced the speaker.

I AM VERY happy to welcome you to our annual dinner. Today is a special occasion for many reasons. First, we are celebrating our seventieth anniversary, which, in a country as young as ours, makes us a venerable institution. A copy of the anniversary manual has been provided for all of you.

Second, we are hosts tonight to twelve librarians from other countries, who are visiting ours to find out how we and our libraries operate. In the interests of international amity, I am going to refrain from doing violence to the names of our guests. Instead, I will ask them to rise and introduce themselves. Will the librarian from Argentina please rise. Brazil, Ceylon, Egypt, Finland, Greece, Guatemala, Honduras, Mexico, The Netherlands, Panama. We are sincerely pleased to have you with us and hope you will see New Yorkers as we really are — friendly, approachable, and eager to help.

We come now to the attraction that drew two hundred of you to this dinner. In introducing a man of our speaker's caliber, the introducer has to fight a tendency to give a blow-by-blow account of his myriad activities. I promise not to do that. I have attended too many dinners where the person making the introduction was captivated by the sound of his own voice, and rambled on and on while his audience grew restless and the hapless speaker grew glassy-eyed.

I will confine myself to one brief story. Many years ago I took a course in penology with a man who had been a Federal inspector of prisons. We were discussing prison riots and one of the students asked the lecturer what started them. The lecturer believed in the Socratic method and turned the question back to the class. Because I always sit in front and try hard to look intelligent, he fixed his gimlet eye on me and said, "Do you know why?" I was much younger then, and afraid to confess I didn't know, so I ventured an answer — "because conditions are unbearable in that prison." I couldn't have given a better answer from the lecturer's point of view because he loved to pounce on wrong ones. "I expected you to say that," he chortled. "It's wrong. Conditions in prison B may be far worse than those in prison A, and yet the riot will occur in A. The answer is that in A there's a leader who makes his fellows aware of and dissatisfied with conditions — who acts as a gadfly."

To us, as thinking people, alive to the dangers inherent in a mummification of opinion, the gadfly is a treasured citizen. Ladies and Gentlemen, I present with pleasure a most articulate gadfly — Harry D. Gideonse.

John Campbell Merriam presents
Ray Lyman Wilbur

John C. Merriam, a distinguished American paleontologist and for many years president of the Carnegie Institution of Washington, presents here Ray Lyman Wilbur (1875–1949), then President of Stanford University.

IT IS GENERALLY said that most of the difficulties occurring among men in the world owe their origin to the fact that we are not able to bring a number of people to see the same thing in the same way. Universities are said to exist for the purpose of giving the broadest and deepest possible view of things as they are, as they have been, and as they are to be. I assume that it is the business of university professors to hold up to the eyes of their students the lens of knowledge so that they may be rid of their intellectual or mental astigmatism and see things in their true position. I assume that it is the business of a faculty to give the students that courage of conviction of the man who sees things as they are and knows that things will stay put. Most of us when we are cowards are cowardly because of uncertainty. The man who goes out from the university should have the clear vision, and by reason of this the strength of conviction, that will enable him to take the initiative.

Stanford University has this clear vision and stands for it. It is a pleasure to us to have with us its president, to talk to us concerning results of research and their application as he may see fit to describe them — President Wilbur.

John E. Stipp presents

Nathan M. Pusey

Nathan M. Pusey, a former professor of Greek history and President of Lawrence College, became President of Harvard in 1953. He was introduced by John E. Stipp, president of the Federal Home Loan Bank of Chicago at a meeting of the Executives' Club of Chicago, October 29, 1954.

HARVARD UNIVERSITY has had twenty-three consecutive presidents born and raised in New England. It has had twenty-two presidents who were Bostonians. From that, you might say that a kind of tradition had developed.

But last year the oldest university in the United States broke this tradition and picked its twenty-fourth president — a man who was born and raised in Council Bluffs, Iowa, and who was President of Wisconsin's Lawrence College at the time of his election to the presidency of Harvard.

The President of Brown University, Henry Wriston, when he was President of Lawrence, noted that he had on his faculty "the most brilliant young teacher I have ever known." This brilliant young teacher, who had worked his way across the country to California and back, teaching, was Nathan Marsh Pusey, our guest speaker today.

President Pusey, of the Harvard class of '28, *magna cum laude*, has studied in Europe, and has a master's and doctorate degree from Harvard, specializing in ancient history and Athenian civilization. Incidentally, he wrote his doctorate paper in the Greek language. From all this you will readily see that he is an outstanding scholar. He has taught at Lawrence, Riverdale Country School, Scripps College at Claremont, California, and Wesleyan University.

He did a remarkable job as President of Lawrence, in the fields of both school studies and the endowment fund, which almost doubled under his leadership.

A Wisconsin reporter, upon the occasion of Dr. Pusey's receiving the news of his new appointment as President of Harvard, wrote that when the students serenaded him that night, he told them, "I don't want you to think that we're going to a better college. That's not true. It's bigger, but not essentially better."

Well, it certainly was bigger, with ten thousand students compared to eight hundred; with an endowment of $210 million compared to $2.5 million.

A national magazine quoted President Pusey's philosophy of higher education in these words:

Christopher Fry said recently that "affairs are now soul-sized." The American colleges must recognize this fact, and remember again that the true business of liberal education is greatness. It is our task not to produce "safe" men, in whom our safety can never, in any case, lie, but to keep alive in young people the courage to dare to seek the truth, to be free, to establish in them a compelling desire to live greatly and magnanimously, and to give them the knowledge and awareness, the faith and the trained facility, to get on with the job. Especially the faith, for as someone has said, the whole world now looks to us for a creed to believe and a song to sing. The whole world — and our young people first of all.

Gentlemen, to discuss the question "What's Going On at Harvard" I present President Pusey.

Frank S. Streeter presents
Frederick S. Jones

Frank S. Streeter, a distinguished lawyer and trustee of Dartmouth College, introduced Dean Jones of Yale University, who was the principal speaker at the inauguration of Ernest Martin Hopkins as President of Dartmouth College, October 6, 1916.

GENTLEMEN: In order that we may be enabled to hear our friend Dean Jones of Yale, who is obliged to catch an early train, I shall ask him to speak next. In doing so, while I would like to say many nice things about him, I will restrain myself as I do not want to take up his time. I introduce him not only as a great college administrator, but also as a poet. Some Boston gentleman — of course, it was a Harvard graduate — tossed off this effusion:

> I come from good old Boston,
>> The home of the bean and the cod,
> Where the Cabots speak only to Lowells,
>> And the Lowells speak only to God.

This was carried down to New Haven, and Dean Jones with the spirit of poetry bubbling up in him, and to illustrate the absolute democracy of Yale, replied:

> Here's to the town of New Haven,
>> The home of the truth and the light,
> Where God talks to Jones in the very same tones
>> That he uses to Hadley and Dwight.

I present Dean Jones, administrator and poet.

Melvin Brorby presents
Arnold J. Toynbee

Arnold J. Toynbee, distinguished professor of the philosophy of history, completed his famous *Study of History* in 1954 in ten volumes. Later he added an atlas and gazetteer (volume 11, 1959) and a final volume entitled *Reconsiderations* (volume 12, 1961). A condensed version of the set became a best seller. Actively interested all his life in international relations, Toynbee was introduced on this occasion by Melvin Brorby, president of the Chicago Council on Foreign Relations.

GOOD AFTERNOON, Ladies and Gentlemen: I am sure I don't need to tell you that this is a gala occasion. I have decided to omit the usual announcements of coming Council activities. But it would break my official Council heart if I did not extend to all of you who are not already members, an invitation to join the Council on Foreign Relations. Out of this sea of shining faces, I am sure there are at least a few of you who would like to join us. To anyone who has the slightest impulse in this direction, I urge you to follow it recklessly! You will find application forms in the lobby and young ladies to answer your questions.

It is always a pleasure to introduce the distinguished guests at our speakers' table, but especially so today.

If I seem a little wiser-looking to you today, it's of course because of the privilege of sitting next to Professor Toynbee. What a fine and civilizing thing it would be if wisdom and vision were more contagious — but actually, and fortunately to a certain extent, this really is so, as you will experience yourselves within the hour.

The name of Arnold Toynbee has been something to conjure with, among intellectual circles, for a very long time. For he has set a tremendously high mark in the world of scholarship. But how wonderful it is that his magic has spread far beyond the boundaries of erudition!

Why is this? Many reasons, perhaps, but isn't this one of them? . . .
Into a world that has specialized in analysis, the taking of things
apart, he has brought a genius for synthesis, the putting of things together. And so, instead of the trees, we see the forest! And rising
higher and higher, we see the setting, the forest in the whole world
— and life itself as a whole thing. For that rare gift, Dr. Toynbee, we
thank you.

Arnold J. Toynbee first became interested in international affairs
while he was a student in the British Archaeological School in Ath-
ens. He has never turned back from that interest, particularly in the
world history that lies behind. This has led him to produce 3,150,000
words, now bound into a ten-volume set called *A Study of History*.

In 1921, Dr. Toynbee first set down the plan for the *Study*. The
notes he wrote on half a sheet of paper listed about a dozen headings. These headings stand with very little change as the titles of the
thirteen parts now published in ten volumes.

The last four volumes, just published, have special interest and impact, because in them he sums up his views of society as a whole and
states his strongly felt conclusions about the purpose and meaning
of history and the future of Western civilization.

We are fortunate indeed to have him here today speaking on a
subject of vital interest to every one of us, "World Peace and World
History." Dr. Toynbee.

Charles Martin *presents*
McGeorge Bundy

The Rev. Charles Martin, headmaster of St. Albans School for Boys, Washington, D.C., presented McGeorge Bundy, president of the Ford Foundation, at the annual convention of the Middle States Association of Colleges and Secondary Schools, 1966.

THIS FIRST part of our session today is devoted to an address by Mr. McGeorge Bundy. I need not do more than present him to you because all that he is and all that he has done are very well known to you. He was a Phi Beta Kappa at Yale and then went into the service. There he did distinguished work with Secretary of War Stimson. He went to Harvard as a professor and then dean of the college, and then to distinguished service under two Presidents. Now he is directing one of the great forces and powers of the modern world.

I can't tell you anything about the public life of Mr. Bundy, but perhaps I can tell you something about his private life because his small boys went to St. Albans School. Those of you who have taught small boys know that they are very spontaneous, natural, revealing human beings; and they sometimes reveal that which goes on, that which they think about Dad and that which they think about Mom with remarkably disarming frankness and honesty.

I am glad and happy to be able to say to you that all that the Bundy boys revealed was just the finest, and we saw through them and in them a very hard-working, very conscientious, very able man.

I might also say that as Headmaster I found him a very cooperative parent. St. Albans isn't always wise and has some inflexible rules. It doesn't take lightly, for example, absences from school. We think absences are a condescension to the weakness of the human flesh which we don't like to recognize, even for illness. When at the end of Mr. Bundy's tour of duty he came to me with such respect for the inflexible practices that we have, and for St. Albans, I could only accede at once gladly and happily to any wishes he had.

Looking through a prayer book I happened on a statement which to me was interesting, particularly when I saw the name at the end of the statement. "I believe in the dignity of the individual, in government by law, in respect for the truth, and in a good God. These beliefs are worth my life and more." And the name was McGeorge Bundy.

I showed the statement to Mr. Bundy and he said that it belongs to his youth. I know he wrote it shortly after he left college, but I think it has been exemplified in his life and we can recognize it.

I am very happy to present to you one who has given all his life, and certainly a very able life, to education and to public service, and is now here to share some of that life with us.

Mr. Bundy.

John G. Milburn presents
James R. Day

James Roscoe Day, Chancellor of Syracuse University from 1893 to 1922, was introduced by John G. Milburn, president of the Economic Club of New York, when he spoke at the seventeenth annual meeting of the Club, November 22, 1911.

GENTLEMEN: From the middle of the fourteenth century to the beginning of the nineteenth century there were slightly over two hundred acts passed by the British Parliament regulating trade and commerce, and combinations in restraint of trade and prices, and every other subject in any other way or degree pertaining to trade or commerce.

A characteristic and interesting feature, too, of that legislation is that the preamble of almost every new act declares that the previous act which it proceeds to repeal has worked exactly the contrary effect to what had been expected. I do not know now but that in the not distant future we will have an act of Congress with a preamble reciting that the enforcement of the Sherman Act has legalized combinations in restraint of trade, tending to produce a monopoly, and therefore be it enacted it is repealed, and all such agreements that are deemed to be improper, to be hereafter authorized.

I am not prophesying; so I will call upon an educational leader who has devoted his life, as a student and observer, to political and economic questions. I introduce to you Chancellor James R. Day of Syracuse University.

Louis Nizer presents
Harry Woodburn Chase

Harry Woodburn Chase served successively as President of the University of North Carolina, President of the University of Illinois, and Chancellor of New York University. He is introduced here by Louis Nizer, prominent New York lawyer, whose fascinating book of courtroom stories and tactics, *My Life in Court*, was published in 1961.

THE DEVELOPMENT of science has embraced pedagogy. Someone once described a lecture as the process by which the notes of the professor passed to the pupil without passing through the brains of either of them.

President Lowell of Harvard expressed a similar skeptical view when he said there must be a great deal of knowledge in our universities because the freshmen always bring a little bit in and the seniors never take any of it out.

Even our own Dr. Nicholas Murray Butler has joined the skeptics by suggesting the following epitaph for the average man: "Dead at thirty — buried at sixty."

Stephen Leacock offered this idea for education: "If I were founding a university I would found first a smoking room; then a dormitory. Then, when I had a little money in hand, I would establish a decent reading room and a library. After that, if I still had some money I couldn't use, I would get some textbooks and hire a professor."

But it was President Hutchins of Chicago University who expressed the ultramodern view of education. He said, "My idea of education is to unsettle the minds of the young and inflame their intellects."

The distinguished scholar whom I now introduce to you has made a happy compromise between the old tradition of teaching and the

91

modern scientific devices of encouraging independent thought.

Some day we will realize that the generals of our educational institutions lead more important armies than those who head the infantry and the cavalry.

I introduce to you the Chancellor of New York University — Professor Harry Woodburn Chase!

Henry Hill presents Francis B. Haas

Francis B. Haas, state superintendent of public instruction in Pennsylvania, was introduced at the opening session of the twenty-fourth meeting of the Representative Assembly of the National Education Association, held in Pittsburgh, July 4, 1944, by Henry Hill, superintendent of the Pittsburgh schools.

I AM REMINDED that no introduction, and certainly one that is not even on the program, should be too long. I don't know who said it, but it was something like this: an introduction to be immortal did not have to be eternal and in view of the amount of shock, mental and physical, and everything you are going to have in the next two, three days, I suggest to myself that I be brief!

Our state superintendent has served in a good many capacities in public-school systems of Pennsylvania. He has been a college president and served in several capacities in the state department of public instruction. I am quite sure that neither the constitution nor the statutes of Pennsylvania say that a man has to be a Republican or that just because the governor is a Republican, the state superintendent of public instruction who is appointed by him has to be a Republican. I do have a hunch, however, that a good Republican would stand a better chance.

It was my pleasure to introduce him to the first gathering in Harrisburg after his appointment for the second four-year term. My reason for mentioning the fact that he is a Republican is not to do him any harm or injustice or to give him undue credit of any kind, but simply to mention that he was the well-nigh unanimous choice of both Republicans and Democrats. That is quite a different matter.

It is both an honor and a pleasure to present to you the leader of public education in the Commonwealth of Pennsylvania, the Honorable Francis B. Haas, state superintendent of public instruction.

Helen H. Waller presents
Bertrand Russell

Author, philosopher, mathematician, and recipient of the Nobel Prize for Literature, Bertrand Russell spoke at the first session of the twentieth annual forum of the *New York Herald Tribune*, October 22, 1951. He was introduced by Mrs. Helen H. Waller, director of the forum and presiding chairman on this occasion.

INTRODUCING Bertrand Russell to this audience is almost superfluous; you already know so much about him; and his life work symbolizes the subject of this Forum.

So I asked him what he would most like to have me tell you. He suggested that I remind you that he is a Socialist supporter of the British Labour government; that he cares more about individual liberty than any other one thing; that on this ground, above all others, he opposes communism and always has. You might call him a premature anti-Communist, since he lost most of his influential friends in the 1920's by his hatred and outspoken criticism of the Russian Communist dictatorship.

Moscow most often refers to him as a "wolf in a dinner jacket." Lord Russell seldom wears a dinner jacket, but he wanted me to tell you that as far as tonight is concerned, the Moscow statement is a half-truth.

Some of you may remember the accident a few years ago when Lord Russell was flying from Oslo to Trondheim. His plane crashed in a fjord, nineteen of the forty passengers were killed. The others, including Lord Russell, swam to safety. When he got to his hotel room the phone rang. It was a reporter asking him, "As the plane was sinking, did you think about mysticism and logic?" "No," came the reply. "What did you think about?" "I thought the water was cold." Later,

Lord Russell commented, "I guess this was the only way to get a drink of brandy in Norway on a Sunday."

Next Wednesday evening Lord Russell will open the 1951 lecture series of Columbia University's Institute of the Arts and Sciences.

When he received the Nobel Prize for Literature earlier this year, Lord Russell was cited by the award committee as "one of our most brilliant specimens of rationality and humanity and a virile champion of free speech and free thought in the West." He is one of the great philosophers of our day, Bertrand Russell.

Frank Porter Graham *presents*
Robert M. Hutchins

Robert M. Hutchins, president of the Fund for the Republic, at the time Chancellor of the University of Chicago, was introduced at the May 5, 1948, meeting of the National Association of State Universities by Frank Porter Graham, United Nations representative for India and Pakistan and former President of the University of North Carolina.

GENTLEMEN, we are very fortunate to have our speaker of the evening. I am not going to introduce him. I am just going to make two statements — that any university that has as much to do with making the atomic bomb as the University of Chicago has got the moral responsibility to do something about it; and that before the atomic bomb fell on Japan, many years before that, an atomic bomb fell on the United States of America and his name is Robert M. Hutchins!

Nicholas Murray Butler presents
Wilbur L. Cross

Wilbur L. Cross (1862–1948) served as professor of English at Yale, editor of the *Yale Review*, and governor of Connecticut for a four-term period. One of the principal speakers at the dinner meeting of the American Academy of Arts and Letters, November 13, 1930, he was introduced by Dr. Nicholas Murray Butler, then President of Columbia University.

To BRING this truly remarkable evening to an end, I turn with the beneficent aid of a protective tariff to domestic industry; but to present this domestic industry properly, I must first chide forty-seven American commonwealths. They have missed their opportunity. They have not chosen a governor from the membership of this Academy.

The exercises which have marked today and which will mark tomorrow had to be carefully planned over many months and every detail studied and arranged. The Academy's representative and agent in all that matter, the chairman of our Committee of Arrangements, found time to do it all and nevertheless to get himself elected governor of Connecticut. What that Commonwealth denied to Mark Twain and even to William Gillette, despite his vigor, they have offered to Wilbur Cross, man-of-letters, editor, critic, scholar, beloved university teacher, distinguished member of this Academy, who will for two years divide his time between us and the *Yale Review* and the public business of the state of Connecticut.

Harold O. McLain presents David Seabury

David Seabury, celebrated consulting psychologist, author, and lecturer, was introduced by Harold O. McLain when he appeared before the Executives' Club of Chicago, April 17, 1942. Mr. McLain, Chicago businessman, was serving as president of the Club at this time.

It is, of course, an obvious truism that the most important components of our world are those elements whose mysteries are the most difficult to pierce and chart. The first is God whom every thoughtful man recognizes but no wise man can translate to a purely mundane equation. The element of mystery second in importance to our life is the human soul and its fellow the human mind, the mechanics of which have baffled the world from the beginning.

Physical, social, and political science have run the gamut of varied progress for two thousand years but psychology, the knowledge and natural history of the mind, has probably made more progress in the last fifty years than in all preceding centuries. Now faintly we begin to catch inspirational glimpses of the wonder and beauty and divinity of the human mind.

There are wise men who contribute to the scientific knowledge of the mind and who, even more, apply their intimacy with psychology to helpful and strengthening procedures with their fellow men. Such an eminent consulting and applied psychologist is Mr. David Seabury, our speaker today.

Of course, you remember that Mr. Seabury has appeared before this Executives' Club now for the fifth time. Each time has been a delightful, stimulating, educational experience for us. You know that he is an author of books whose scientific depths are so delightfully leavened with simplicity that we unenlightened laymen can enjoy as well as learn in their reading. You await impatiently, I know, the development of his subject, "Understanding Our Times," which Mr. David Seabury brings to us today, so I shall delay him and you no longer.

Virgil M. Hancher presents

Franklyn Bliss Snyder

At the State University of Iowa, June 19, 1949, President Virgil M. Hancher presented the commencement speaker, Dr. Franklyn B. Snyder, President of Northwestern University.

I HAVE the honor of presenting to this audience a great teacher and a great administrator. President Snyder received his undergraduate degree at Beloit College and his Ph.D. from Harvard University. Immediately thereafter he received an appointment at Northwestern University, and he has served that institution in the successive ranks and positions of instructor, assistant professor, associate professor, professor, Graduate Dean, Vice President and Dean of the Faculties, and President of the University.

His general field of teaching, research and writing was in English literature, and his special field was the life, personality, character, and art of Robert Burns — a subject in which he achieved national and international recognition.

Every university has a few courses so outstanding that they are in effect required courses — and they are made so by the spontaneous recognition of students, whatever the university requirements may be. Dr. Snyder's course in English literature was such a course. That he was an outstanding teacher I have from the personal testimony of Mrs. Hancher, who was privileged to be one of his students.

This year Dr. Snyder completes forty years of continuous service to Northwestern, the last ten as President of the University. Having reached the statutory age, he will retire this year with the rewarding knowledge that under his presidency Northwestern University has become one of the greatest of our universities and one of the most soundly financed among the privately endowed universities.

In a few days Dr. and Mrs. Snyder will leave for a trip to Europe

— a project in which he will have not only our good wishes, but perhaps a bit of our envy as well. Any president who has served his university ably and faithfully for a period of ten years, encompassing both war and its aftermath, has well earned a trip to Europe. I trust that this precedent will not be overlooked in other cases!

He will return next autumn in full vigor of mind and body to enter upon another task of rigorous activity and responsible public service.

I take pleasure in presenting to this audience my distinguished friend, Dr. Franklyn Bliss Snyder, President of Northwestern University. President Snyder.

JOURNALISM

Hedley Donovan presents
Henry R. Luce

Henry R. Luce (1898–1967), editor and publisher, was honored at a *Yale Daily News* banquet April 21, 1965. The main speaker on this occasion was Hedley Donovan, Editor-in-Chief of Time Inc. At the conclusion of his talk on the subject of change as it confronts the journalist, he presented Mr. Luce as "one of the most perceptive students of change."

So MUCH for my half dozen glimpses of the journalist grappling with change. I hope I have relieved Harry Luce of any anxiety that I might spend all evening talking about him. But I am sure all the rest of you recognize that in talking about change I am not really digressing very far from the main business of this dinner. For the man we are saluting this evening is one of the most perceptive students of change and one of the most vigorous fomenters of change that this restless nation of ours has ever produced.

Last year a competitive publication — I will mention its name, the *Saturday Evening Post* — commissioned a long profile of Mr. Luce. I was one of dozens of people interviewed by the writer. I spent several hours talking to him, and furnished him, free of charge, with a number of valuable insights into the mind and character of Henry Luce. When the article appeared, I found the writer had used none of my insights, and furthermore I found myself described, for my pains, as "taciturn."

What I had tried mainly to convey to the writer was some feeling of Henry Luce's extraordinary zest for new ideas, not only as inspiration for new modes and vehicles of journalism, but as subject matter for journalism. Far from being pained by new ideas, as Walter Bagehot says men are, Henry Luce rejoices in them. He has thought up some himself, which is rare enough, and perhaps rarer still in men of truly original minds, he delights in meeting with other men's new ideas. He welcomes argument so ardently that it takes a certain amount of intellectual courage to agree with him when he is right, as is bound to happen from time to time. I remember once some years ago, as a junior *Fortune* writer, startling some of my fellow junior *Fortune* writers over the lunch table, by announcing the thesis that the boss is not always wrong. Having since become a boss of sorts myself, I am glad to have this statement on record so long ago.

Along with Harry Luce's exceptional creativity and curiosity — the intellectual welcome he extends to so many forms of change and possibilities of change — he has a steadfast devotion to the principles that do not change. I hope I do not create any embarrassment in this sophisticated gathering if I describe those principles, very simply, as faith in his country and faith in his God. The faith seems not to fight with the intellect, but to inform and enliven it; Henry Luce has integrity not only in the sense of honesty but in the sense of wholeness. He believes that the changes of our age have meaning, that we are capable of working changes for the better, indeed, that this is required of us. I think he would also say, as a journalist and as an American, that we ain't seen anything yet.

It is surely a redundancy for me to be "introducing" Henry Luce to a Yale gathering. But it is one of the most agreeable redundancies that has ever befallen me, and I thank the *Yale Daily News* for bringing it about. May I present to you, then, your former Managing Editor, your present Chubb Fellow, my own boss, tutor, and very dear friend of many years, Henry Luce.

Louis Nizer presents

Heywood Broun

Heywood Broun (1888–1939) started his journalistic career with the *New York Tribune* and the *New York World*. He was a consistent opponent of social injustice. The introduction is by Louis Nizer, prominent New York lawyer, whose fascinating book of courtroom stories and tactics, *My Life in Court*, was published in 1961.

I AM GOING to introduce to you a newspaper columnist not funny enough to be a gag man — not serious enough to be an editorial commentator.

I am going to introduce to you a critic not severe enough to be the producers' anathema — not generous enough to be charged with prejudice because he was once an actor himself.

I am going to introduce to you an actor who, despite his bulk, has never been able to play heavy parts — and who, when he essayed light parts, almost realized his ambition of being a tragedian.

I am going to introduce to you a producer who has not lost enough money in the theatre to deserve that designation — and who has not produced a sufficient number of plays to justify a future failure on the ground of past success.

I am going to introduce to you a radio speaker who doesn't talk fast enough to give the public its money's worth according to the present standard of an avalanche of words — and who doesn't talk melodiously enough to attract a female audience even if it doesn't understand what he says.

I am going to introduce to you a socialist — not radical enough to be called by his malicious enemies a Bolshevik — not conservative enough to be called even by his malicious friends a pink liberal.

I am going to introduce to you a philosopher — not profound

enough to be an academician — not agrarian enough to be home-spun.

I am going to introduce to you a writer whose facility of expression, velvety style, and wisdom make him the most consistently interesting writer in all newspaperdom.

I am going to introduce to you a man whose sagacity, with righteous indignation and clear thinking, reveals the lunacy of the world around us.

I am going to introduce to you *all* of these men — Heywood Broun!

Henry R. Spencer presents
Anne O'Hare McCormick

Anne O'Hare McCormick, who served as a member of the editorial board of the *New York Times* until her death in 1954, was awarded a Pulitzer prize for distinguished reporting as a foreign correspondent in 1937. She is presented here by Professor Henry R. Spencer, professor emeritus of the Department of Political Science of Ohio State University.

IF THIS be a man's world, we have surely made a mess of it. But as we are young we are resolved to learn, and we turn therefore to the other sex.

We all got the first part of our training at mother's knee, and if that influence had been more continued and by us cherished and developed, our mess would have been less. Most of us as American schoolchildren were under the tuition of women, some of whom we value increasingly as our judgment grows more mature.

There are other figures, farther back, in literature. In the comedy of Aristophanes, centuries before Christ, we had Lysistrata, giving a woman's counsel as to how war could be brought to an end. In the same period Aeschylus, Sophocles, and especially Euripides gave us the figure of Antigone, with her profound, poignant preachment on the nature of justice and law.

Coming to our own day, permit the calling of certain witnesses whose testimony has brought enlightenment, at least to me. There is Señora Isabel de Palencia, statesman and diplomat of republican Spain, with her stirring autobiography entitled *I Must Have Liberty*. There is the Italian educator, Maria Montessori, with her two friends and interpreters, Mme. Fischbacher translating to the French, and our own Dorothy Canfield introducing Montessori ideas to the English-reading world. There is Baroness Ishimoto and her book of a decade and a half ago, *Facing Two Ways*, with its wistful interpreta-

107

tion of her beloved America to her beloved Japan, and vice versa. There is Vera Dean, Russian-born, American-trained, who is the heart and soul, and especially the brain, of that precious educational institution, the Foreign Policy Association.

And then there is the distinguished lady whom it is our privilege to welcome this evening. Columbus points with pride to her local origin, and education at St. Mary of the Springs. This university is proud of having an occasion which, she may remember, was favored by the presence of Olympian deity, Jupiter Pluvius et Tonans, letting us have a downpour which almost set the stadium afloat.

As valued columnist-commentator long before that term had suffered deflation, as Pulitzer Prize winner, and especially as member of the editorial council of the *New York Times,* she has become an indispensable instrument of our political education, notable for trenchant penetration in style, and for sagacity in judgment.

I give you Mrs. Anne O'Hare McCormick, whose theme is "Europe and Ourselves."

Richard T. Cragg presents
Chet Huntley

At the September 30, 1966, meeting of the Executives' Club of Chicago, the noted NBC news correspondent Chet (Chester Robert) Huntley spoke on the power and prestige of the United States in world affairs. He was introduced by Richard T. Cragg, president of the Club.

BACK IN the 1920's when Chet Huntley attended grammar school and high school, the heroes and heroines were found on the local movie screens at the Saturday matinees. Now some thirty-five years later, we find Chet himself the idol in millions of homes throughout this country. His unusual and interesting style of news presentation and analysis, both alone and with his teammate, David Brinkley, has brought him national fame.

Chester Robert Huntley was born in Cardwell, Montana, in 1911, the son of a rancher and railroad telegrapher. In 1932, Chet won a national oratory contest at Montana State, where he was enrolled. The prize was a scholarship to the Cornish School of Arts in Seattle, where he abandoned an earlier ambition to study medicine and decided upon speech and drama.

He later graduated from the University of Washington and joined a Seattle radio station. Like many radio staffers, he did more jobs than one, even sweeping up the studio on occasion.

In 1955 he joined NBC and from then on, most all of us have heard a great deal from Chet Huntley. His interesting and unique coverage of national political conventions immediately won him nationwide popularity, and he and his associate, David Brinkley, enjoyed wide praise from television critics and audiences, and the ratings quickly reflected this popularity.

In addition to many awards won by the "Huntley-Brinkley Report," Chet has received numerous honors for his individual re-

109

porting. Among these was the Alfred I. Dupont Award as Commentator of the Year.

And so in true television style I say, "Good night, David" — no, I mean, "Take it away, Chet."

Elihu Root presents

Henry Watterson

Henry Watterson, distinguished orator, editor, and writer, was manager and editor of the *Louisville Courier-Journal* from 1868 to 1919. He was introduced by the winner of the Nobel Prize for Peace in 1912, Elihu Root, at a banquet of the New England Society, December 22, 1894.

GENTLEMEN: We are forced to recognize the truth of the observation that all the people of New England are not puritans; we must admit an occasional exception. It is equally true, I am told, that all the people of the South are not cavaliers; but there is one cavalier without fear and without reproach, the splendid courage of whose convictions shows how close together the highest examples of different types can be among godlike men — a cavalier of the South, of southern blood and southern life, who carries in thought and in deed all the serious purpose and disinterested action that characterized the Pilgrim Fathers whom we commemorate. He comes from an impressionist state, where the grass is blue, where the men are either all black or all white, and where, we are told, quite often the settlements are painted red. He is a soldier, a statesman, a scholar, and, above all, a lover; and among all the world which loves a lover, the descendants of those who, generation after generation, with tears and laughter, have sympathized with John Alden and Priscilla, cannot fail to open their hearts in sympathy to Henry Watterson and his star-eyed goddess. I have the honor and great pleasure of introducing him to respond to the toast of "The Puritan and the Cavalier."

Mrs. William B. Meloney presents

Dorothy Thompson

Dorothy Thompson (1894–1961), one of the most widely read commentators of world affairs, began her journalistic career in London for *International News*, and her subsequent work for American newspapers during the rise of nazism put her among the principal foreign correspondents. She was introduced by Mrs. William B. Meloney, editor of *This Week*, as one of the speakers at the fifth annual forum of the *New York Herald Tribune*, October 15, 1935.

OF ALL the women in American life, the one best known and most feared by European politicians is Dorothy Thompson. She has the wit to see, the passion to learn, and the courage to speak. In those countries where men are reluctant to grant importance to women on their own account, she has been saluted as the wife of Sinclair Lewis, which has highly amused him, because he thinks she is sufficient as a person in herself.

By some writers she has been called "a blue-eyed tornado." Witty, wise, warm-hearted, she has won many friends and a large following of readers. She went to Russia, studied it, and wrote one of the best books on the Soviet, so good that one of America's best sellers copied considerable of it without credit. She went to Germany, expressed her opinions and was ordered out by Hitler. She has contributed important articles on world affairs to the *Saturday Evening Post* and other publications, and she is sought by lecture bureaus all over the land. She knows a great deal about foreign governments and even more about her own. She has studied the effects of propaganda and has been a dispassionate observer. For all of these reasons and because women can with pride accept her word and her guidance, we have asked her to close this session on what has been called the highly dangerous subject of propaganda. She will speak to you on "Government by Propaganda." Miss Dorothy Thompson.

Thomas H. Coulter presents
Marguerite Higgins

Marguerite ("Maggie") Higgins (1920–1966), ace correspondent on the Korean battlefront, was introduced at the February 23, 1951, meeting of the Executives' Club of Chicago by its president, Thomas H. Coulter.

WHEN MAGGIE HIGGINS arrived at the Korean battlefront two days after the Communist invasion, she had no idea that her daring reporting would catapult her to international fame. Instead of writing headlines she herself became one almost overnight, when General Walker bounced her out of Korea with the advice that a war was no place for a woman.

She protested to General MacArthur that she was not working in Korea as a woman but as a war correspondent, and put up such a good front about why she should be at the front that he granted her a reprieve.

In spite of all her efforts to conceal her womanly attributes in baggy pants, oversize shirts and a solid covering of Korean dust, the GI's haven't been fooled and one admiring observer remarked, "Maggie wears mud like other women wear makeup."

Miss Higgins owes her physical properties to an Irish-American father and a French mother, who became a war bride after meeting her father as a combat flyer in World War I. Mr. Higgins became a globe-trotting businessman, which resulted in Maggie being born in Hong Kong. She spoke only French and Chinese until the age of twelve. After schooling in France, she attended the University of California where she graduated with honors.

She became a *Herald Tribune* campus correspondent while working for her master's degree in journalism at Columbia, and in 1942 joined the paper's New York staff.

Two years later, Miss Higgins got the chance she had been asking for. Because of her fluency in French, the *Herald Tribune* sent her to Europe as a war correspondent.

There she covered Buchenwald and reported the capture of Munich and the liberation of Dachau and Berchtesgaden. For the last two of these stories, she was given the New York Newspaper Women's Club award for the best foreign correspondent of 1945. The same year, at age twenty-four, she became chief of the paper's Berlin Bureau.

After three years of able postwar reporting in Germany, she became the *Trib's* Tokyo Bureau chief last June, and was one of the first reporters to get to Korea when the war started.

She has been at the fighting front almost continuously since then, and has retreated in defeat and advanced in victory from Pusan to the Manchurian border where she was trapped with the marines at the Changjin reservoir.

Her disregard for personal safety would have warmed the heart of Ernie Pyle. Once when she was not heard from for several days, it turned out that she had landed with the fifth wave of marines at Inchon, and stayed with them under intense mortar and machine gun fire until that beach was secured.

All this has made "news-chick" Higgins a sort of GI heroine, won her the universal affection of the troops, and endeared her to millions of readers.

The question of what makes Maggie run so hard and fast, fascinates her three hundred male competitors in Korea almost as much as the war itself. She has forced these who at first regarded her as an impudent upstart in the business of reporting battles to admit grudgingly that she was their match when it came to bravery and scoops.

She is a symbol of the courage and intelligence that sets apart the great war correspondent from the routine reporter.

We are privileged to hear her make her first public address.

Ladies and Gentlemen: Miss Marguerite Higgins.

Lee Hills *presents*
Fred Sparks

Speaking before the Economic Club of Detroit, February 25, 1952, Fred Sparks, roving correspondent of the *Chicago Daily News* Foreign Service, was introduced by Lee Hills, executive editor of the *Detroit Free Press*.

It was just twenty months ago today that the war began in Korea — and it was just eight months ago today that Mr. Malik suggested that we talk about how to stop the shooting. That means that we have been negotiating for more than one third of the total time of the war. And if the talks go on just a few more months, it will mean that we have talked about stopping it as long as we fought it without talking before.

So what goes on? Are the Communists delaying — stalling while they prepare another attack? Just what sort of a war is it? Was General MacArthur right? I think our speaker today, Fred Sparks, can answer some of these questions, and he will limit his address so there will be time for questions.

Fred was at the peace talks representing the Knight Newspapers and *Chicago Daily News* Foreign Service. I know you have all seen the announcement and read about the assignments that he has had all over the world. He has been on the go outside of this country for the last eight years, since he was a war correspondent in World War II. Right now he is back in this country on a sabbatical.

He came to Detroit — the first time he had ever been here — last December — and liked it. He visited tank plants, truck plants, and other factories. He saw in Detroit the arsenal of the fighting machine that he has lived with overseas. He wanted to work again in a news room. He wanted to talk with the people at home, so he could learn better how to write for us when he goes back overseas. He wanted to find out what the people at home are thinking of our efforts abroad.

I persuaded Fred to spend his sabbatical working with us on the *Free Press,* and we are proud to call him a colleague.

Fred has spent more time with our GI's in Korea than any other correspondent. He has lived with them, he has shared their rations, their problems, and he has heard their gripes. He intended to abide by the Geneva Convention which, as you know forbids correspondents from carrying weapons; that is, he intended to until one night when the Chinese Reds surrounded a Marine company he was with. When they broke out, Fred was carrying a carbine, and he said, "Well, if an armed Communist jumps into my foxhole, what am I supposed to do? Do I reach in my pocket and pull out my press card and shout '*Free Press* Correspondent' ?"

The list of hot spots that Fred has covered is far longer than the one that you have read in the folder. He has done so much traveling by air and ship and train and dog sled and camel caravan and just plain shanks' mare that he left twelve different countries before his laundry was returned.

All of these things have happened to Mr. Sparks before his thirty-seventh birthday. When I asked him the other day why he wasn't married, he said, "Well, Lee, a few girls I nominated for the job of Mrs. Sparks declined. They thought that if my laundry couldn't catch up with me, how could they?"

It is my privilege and great pleasure to present one of the greatest of that group of correspondents whose job it is to explain the vast events now shaping our lives and fortunes, a reporter of great skill and integrity, and a man completely devoted to his country — Fred Sparks.

Samuel L. Clemens presents
Henry M. Stanley

Sir Henry Morton Stanley, Welsh-born explorer, came to this country in 1859 and became a reporter for the *New York Herald* in 1868. Among his most exciting assignments was the search in 1871 for the lost Scottish missionary David Livingstone. He was introduced by Samuel L. Clemens at a meeting in Boston, November 1886. The introduction is reprinted by permission of the copyright owners from *Mark Twain's Speeches, with an Introduction by Albert Bigelow Paine.* Copyright 1923, 1950, by the Mark Twain Company.

LADIES AND GENTLEMEN, if any should ask, Why is it that you are here as introducer of the lecturer? I should answer that I happened to be around and was asked to perform this function. I was quite willing to do so, and, as there was no sort of need of an introduction, anyway, it could be necessary only that some person come forward for a moment and do an unnecessary thing, and this is quite in my line. Now, to introduce so illustrious a name as Henry M. Stanley by any detail of what the man has done is clear aside from my purpose; that would be stretching the unneccessary to an unconscionable degree. When I contrast what I have achieved in my measurably brief life with what he has achieved in his possibly briefer one, the effect is to sweep utterly away the ten-story edifice of my own self-appreciation and leave nothing behind but the cellar. When you compare these achievements of his with the achievements of really great men who exist in history, the comparison, I believe, is in his favor. I am not here to disparage Columbus.

No, I won't do that; but when you come to regard the achievements of these two men, Columbus and Stanley, from the standpoint of the difficulties they encountered, the advantage is with Stanley and against Columbus. Now, Columbus started out to discover

America. Well, he didn't need to do anything at all but sit in the cabin of his ship and hold his grip and sail straight on, and America would discover itself. Here it was, barring his passage the whole length and breadth of the South American continent, and he couldn't get by it. He'd got to discover it. But Stanley started out to find Doctor Livingstone, who was scattered abroad, as you may say, over the length and breadth of a vast slab of Africa as big as the United States.

It was a blind kind of search. He was the worst scattered of men. But I will throw the weight of this introduction upon one very peculiar feature of Mr. Stanley's character, and that is his indestructible Americanism — an Americanism which he is proud of. And in this day and time, when it is the custom to ape and imitate English methods and fashions, it is like a breath of fresh air to stand in the presence of this untainted American citizen who has been caressed and complimented by half of the crowned heads of Europe, who could clothe his body from his head to his heels with the orders and decorations lavished upon him. And yet, when the untitled myriads of his own country put out their hands in welcome to him and greet him, "Well done," through the Congress of the United States, that is the crown that is worth all the rest to him. He is a product of institutions which exist in no other country on earth — institutions that bring out all that is best and most heroic in a man. I introduce Henry M. Stanley.

THE LAW

George Wharton Pepper presents
Earl Warren

Earl Warren became Chief Justice of the United States in 1953, having served previously as Attorney General and later as Governor of California. He was introduced on the occasion of the thirty-third annual meeting of the American Law Institute (1956) by the presiding officer, George Wharton Pepper, distinguished lawyer, leader, and former United States Senator from Pennsylvania.

THE SIGNIFICANCE of these annual meetings throughout the life of the Institute has been due to the presence of a representative of the Supreme Court of the United States. Today we are again thus honored, and presently I shall give you an opportunity to extend a greeting to our distinguished guest.

Meanwhile, it is hardly necessary for me to remind you that he comes to us at a moment in history when the stability of our Republic is again under strain. Our most cherished institution, the Supreme Court, is again under attack. And while experience shows that the justices are abundantly able to take care of themselves, I am sure that they feel that one of their elements of strength is the confidence of the American bar.

I know what can be said in disparagement of republics; and if I did not, I could find among our citizenship a number of people who would be willing and even anxious to point out the deficiency in our own system. At such times I like to encourage myself by recalling an observation by that American patriot, Fisher Ames, who once spoke somewhat as follows:

Said he, "A monarchy is like a full-rigged ship with all sails set, easy to steer and majestic to look upon. But a single stone will send her to the bottom. A republic, on the other hand, is more like the homely raft, sometimes under water and occasionally your feet are wet. But nothing can sink her!"

That is a sentiment we all echo, and I thank God that at this moment in history we may be devoutly grateful for the Supreme Court, and for having at its head a man whose personal integrity, whose tireless energy, and whose imaginative statesmanship qualify him to be the head of our judicial system. Fellow Americans, I ask you to rise in place and extend your greeting to the Chief Justice of the United States!

Harrison Tweed presents

Hartley Shawcross

Sir Hartley W. Shawcross, statesman, lawyer, and Labour member of Parliament, served as chief prosecutor for the United Kingdom at the Nuremberg war crimes trials. He was introduced on the occasion of the thirty-fifth meeting of the American Law Institute (1958) by the presiding officer, Harrison Tweed, prominent New York lawyer.

. . . THIS SPEAKER has had a very distinguished career, as you all know, and I do not need to go into the details of it.

He is a practicing lawyer, has been Attorney General, Member of Parliament, Head of the Board of Trade, and he is now participating in advising and helping, in business and other capacities, one of the big oil companies which does business here and abroad.

In asking this speaker to come, I did not rely exclusively on my desire to have a speaker from Great Britain, or even on my confidence that Great Britain's lawyers are good speakers. I had had the privilege of hearing Sir Hartley Shawcross speak in Texas about twelve years ago.

I remember the occasion very well. I had been invited to speak to the Bar Association of Texas, and I thought that it was a great honor and that I was going to give them a very great speech which they would never forget.

I went down there and found that Sir Hartley Shawcross was having such a good time that he had not left on schedule, and he was going to say a little something to this meeting of the Association.

He made a very good speech. He made a speech of farewell. He was running off to jump on an airplane and go back. But it seemed to me as he got up and left the room, that the whole audience was going to go with him — which was a little disconcerting to me if I was to speak after him.

123

But he spoke briefly, and, in spite of the fact of the letdown, in spite of the fact that the subject of my speech was "Is the Bar Awake or Asleep?"—in spite of the fact that towards the end of the speech it began to be fairly obvious that that part of the bar that was there was pretty fairly sound asleep, I got through the evening without any resentment, rather with gratitude.

On that occasion, as I remember it, Sir Hartley addressed himself very intensively to the ladies. He had the ladies absolutely entranced. In fact, he rather ignored all the gentlemen.

But tonight with Lady Shawcross here—and we are very glad that she is here—I think Sir Hartley may have something to say to the gentlemen.

Sir Hartley Shawcross!

Harrison Tweed presents
Dillon Anderson

Dillon Anderson, a Texas lawyer prominent in national affairs since World War II, is best known to the general public as the creator of two zany characters who first appeared in the *Atlantic Monthly* and later in book form as *I and Claudie* (1951). He is introduced on the occasion of the thirty-fourth annual meeting of the American Law Institute (1957) by the presiding officer, Harrison Tweed, prominent New York lawyer.

I AM NOT going to try to introduce the speaker of the evening in the way in which Senator Pepper would, because nobody else can do that, Senator Pepper. I am only going to tell you a few little things about him.

One of them is that he comes from Texas; probably you all know that, notwithstanding that the woods are full of Texans, particularly the Washington woods. But he is an outstanding man even among the numerous Texans who pervade the atmosphere and walk the corridors of Washington.

He went away from Texas for a short while after he was born, to Oklahoma where he had a college education. Then he went to Yale Law School and got some more education — quite a lot of education, I judge, because the New York law firms tried to restrain him and make him practice law in New York, but he refused to do that, and he went back to Texas.

There he practiced law for quite a while, until he felt the call of the Army, where he served for three years during the Second World War, ended up as a colonel, and had a couple of decorations.

They got him into service as Special Assistant to the President of the United States on National Security Affairs. He went over to the summit conference at Geneva, and acquitted himself as we would expect he would.

He served his time in Washington, nearly killed himself by over-working, and then went back to Texas to the comparative peace of the practice of the law. So much for that part of his career. There is another phase of his life that perhaps you don't all know about. He is a writer of short stories, and very amusing short stories they are. He says that he writes them on the train, but I rather suspect that he writes them during some of the sessions of the American Law Institute.

They are very delightful stories. His characters are rather reckless, lawless characters, who wander around the Texas domain in a kind of happy-go-lucky fashion. I sometimes suspect that there is a little autobiography involved, but the author says no, he is merely drawing on his imagination.

There are two characters in these stories. Of one of them he said, speaking of a particular occasion, "He looks very much worried. That probably means that he is thinking, because he always looks worried when he is thinking."

As I look at him, he does not look very much worried. Maybe that means he is able to think without looking worried, or maybe it means that he isn't thinking. But in any event, he is going to speak to us. If he wanders a little in his talk tonight, that is just the hobo in him, and I am sure we will all enjoy wandering with him.

Mr. Dillon Anderson, of Houston, Texas.

George Wharton Pepper presents
Charles Evans Hughes

Charles Evans Hughes, Chief Justice of the Supreme Court from 1930 to 1941, was one of the Nine Old Men whose invalidation of New Deal laws provoked President Roosevelt's "court-packing" plan of 1937. Before he became Chief Justice, Hughes had been Secretary of State (1921–1925), Republican candidate for President (1916), an Associate Justice of the Supreme Court (1910), and Governor of the State of New York (1907–1908, 1909–1910). On the occasion of the eighteenth annual meeting of the American Law Institute (1940), Chief Justice Hughes was introduced by the presiding officer, George Wharton Pepper, distinguished lawyer, teacher, and former United States Senator from Pennsylvania.

It was said by them of old time that amid the clash of arms the laws are silent: *"inter arma silent leges."* I suggest, however, that even while battle rages we may turn aside for an interval of quiet and consider those things which are the antithesis of chaos. And this we may do without impairing our capacity to act — act in the living present — heart within and God o'erhead.

Before we thus turn aside I am going to ask you all to rise and stand for a brief moment in perfect silence while each in his own way beseeches Almighty God to vindicate His power to order the unruly wills and affections of sinful men.

And now, Ladies and Gentlemen, I bid you welcome to the eighteenth meeting of our American Law Institute and I cheer you with the initial announcement that the presidential address will be omitted.

Last year the Chief Justice was unable to be with us. He was slightly indisposed and had, I believe, been advised that it was best to conserve his strength for the clarification of the commerce clause and other matters about which there is less than unanimity. In his

127

absence, the Court was well represented by Mr. Justice Butler and we established with him so friendly a contact that when he passed on I think each of us felt a sense of personal loss. Today we are happy in having the Chief Justice with us again and I am sure his heart was warmed by the hearty welcome that you gave him. I am not quite sure just how to describe the function which he so happily performs for us. It is not precisely priestly because he has never given us absolution for our mistakes, and it is not wholly prophetic because I notice he has been careful not to commit his Court to blind acceptance of our conclusions. But after all, it is only in the blackletter that we need to be precise. It is enough on this occasion for us to realize that the Chief Justice is with us, that he has shown himself to be a good friend of the Institute and if he cannot with propriety give us either absolution or prophecy, he may at least bestow upon us his blessing. Ladies and Gentlemen, the Chief Justice of the United States.

William Clarke Mason *presents*
George Wharton Pepper

George Wharton Pepper (1867–1961) distinguished lawyer and former United States Senator from Pennsylvania, was introduced by William Clarke Mason, of the law firm of Morgan, Lewis and Bockius, Philadelphia, at the annual banquet of the Pennsylvania Bar Association June 24, 1944. Mr. Mason was president of the Association at the time.

IT SO HAPPENS that every now and then I read a book. It isn't often, because I have to read the briefs that are prepared by my associates to see whether I can understand what they are saying before I go somewhere to talk about them; but one of the books which I read a great many years ago, and which to me is one of the great companions of joy, is a little book, very few pages, very easy to read, very hard to get — but any of you who can get it and carry it with you, I assure you, you will never regret it, whatever it costs you.

It is a book which James M. Barrie wrote — or rather, it was his address at St. Andrews when giving his address as Rector of St. Andrews in 1922. He was talking to the boys who were then graduating, and among them in the audience were all of the boys down to the freshman class — and there are many things in that book which I am not going to read, but I am going to read just two sentences. And, as I usually find in the course of the last few years, at least, that the mentality of those who have written is so superior to mine, that it is much easier to quote than it is to try to put words together when they might express something less worth while than I could have given — but Barrie said this, and he was quoting from Izaak Walton:

Doubtless the Almighty might have created a finer fruit than the strawberry [and remember, this is in England, where strawberries are better than you sometimes get them in the frozen food in this country] but He never did. Doubtless He could have provided us with better fun than hard work, but I don't know what it is.

After all, some lawyers, most lawyers, these days, know that hard work gives you the kind of opportunity to satisfy yourselves, that nothing else can do. Doubtless the Almighty and his dear mother could have produced a better lawyer than George Wharton Pepper, but they did not do it. Doubtless they could have produced a more active citizen than George Wharton Pepper in all of the affairs that he has endeavored to follow through, but neither of them thought about it and neither of them contributed anything to improve upon what he has done. And the Almighty and his dear mother may possibly have created a dearer friend and one more loyal to all that friendship means, than George Wharton Pepper, but they did not do it — and he stands today as the outstanding member of the Pennsylvania Bar Association, for all of the things which the Almighty and his mother failed to make better than he represents.

David A. Simmons presents

Walter S. Fenton

Walter S. Fenton, Vermont lawyer, was a guest speaker at the Texas Bar Association meeting, June 30, 1939. He was introduced on this occasion by David A. Simmons, president of the American Bar Association, 1944–1945, and founder of the *Texas Bar Journal*.

MR. PRESIDENT, Ladies and Gentlemen, the story goes that about 1881 a cattleman in west Texas who happened to be presiding as county judge received a letter that read like this:

Dear Sir: I have been informed that your county is growing. I am a young Republican lawyer from Vermont. I am honest and industrious, and would like to know if your county would be a good place for me to settle.

The cattleman perused it with considerable interest, and he wrote back:

Dear Sir: Your letter at hand. As an honest lawyer, you will have little competition in our county. As a Republican we will promise you the protection of the game laws.

Now the next year the Texas Bar Association was organized, and ever since that time we have been trying to improve the reputation of the lawyer at home and his fellowship with the lawyers abroad. And so fifty-eight years later we come to a day when, as our principal speaker, we ask a lawyer from Vermont to come and deliver to us the principal address.

This gentleman has been president of his state bar, the head of the delegation of that state to the American Bar Association for many years. He has been on the Board of Governors of the American Bar Association for the past three years, and it has been a great privilege for me to serve these last two years with him in that capacity. I had served with him on the old General Council for some years before.

I know him as a speaker of no mean ability, with a voice that can be heard, and a brain to formulate things worth hearing.

Last year he had a serious illness, and at the time when our meeting of the American Bar Association was being held in Cleveland I found, not to my surprise, that not only was he highly respected, but that he was really loved, by the American bar, and when he recovered completely there was great joy among all of his friends. I was most happy when President Powell instructed me to invite him here as the guest of our Association. Many of you men have met Mr. Fenton, because for the last four or five years he has attended the luncheon given at each American Bar meeting by the Texas Society, and we claim him as one of our own.

There is only one note of sadness from me, and that is that his beautiful and charming wife could not accompany him here, because they have a young lady daughter who had other plans in the East. She is a great asset to him, as most of our wives are, and he will probably relate a little story about this invitation, connected with Mrs. Fenton.

As a personal friend, it is a pleasure for me to present Walter S. Fenton, of Vermont, to the best Bar Association in the United States.

John G. Buchanan presents
Augustus N. Hand

Augustus Noble Hand (1869–1954), judge of the United States Circuit Court from 1927 to 1953 was introduced by John G. Buchanan, president of the Pennsylvania Bar Association at the fifty-first annual meeting of the Association, June 28, 1946.

WHEN THE GREAT Oliver Wendell Holmes, Jr., sat upon the Supreme Court bench, some said that there was no Roland for that Oliver. A like remark cannot be made of another Federal tribunal which for nearly two decades has been graced by two great lawyers. Shall I say of the same name? The prophetic parents of one of them christened him "Noble" and the equally prophetic parents of the other christened him "Learned." Each of the children earned the right to both of the appellations; each of them is noble and each of them is learned. The Honorable Augustus Noble Hand had a distinguished career as a student at Phillips Exeter Academy, Harvard College and the Harvard Law School, and has served as president of the Alumni Association of each of those institutions of learning, as an overseer of Harvard University and as a trustee of the Episcopal Theological School at Cambridge. He is a Doctor of Laws of Yale University, of the University of Pennsylvania (represented here by a number of other alumni), of Williams College, of Middlebury College, and of Harvard University. What can be better than that? He practiced for nineteen years in the city of New York, where he was a member of a leading firm. Thirty-two years ago he was appointed United States District Judge by President Wilson, and thirteen years later he was appointed a judge of the Circuit Court of Appeals for the Second Circuit by President Coolidge. For the past ten years he has served as a member of the Council and of the Executive Committee of the American Law Institute, and there are many of us who can testify to the laborious and invaluable services which he has rendered to the Institute. Knowing as I do his great distinction as a scholar, as a jurist, and as a churchman, I was prepared to find that he left no field of learning untouched and that he touched nothing which he did not adorn. However, I was scarcely prepared to find, as I did a little more than a month ago, that he is also an eminent vocalist. Whether he speaks or whether he sings, or whether, to take an Episcopalian middle course, he chants, what he has to say to us, we will, I am sure, attend closely to his winged words.

Josephus Daniels presents
Sir Norman Birkett

Sir Norman Birkett, later Baron Birkett (1883–1962), was concerned with many of the most important criminal cases in England during his years at the bar and on the bench. He was introduced by Josephus Daniels, statesman and newspaper editor, at the forty-fourth annual meeting of the North Carolina Bar Association, May 17, 1942. Another introduction of Sir Norman appears in this book in the section entitled "The Literary World."

MR. PRESIDENT, Members of the Bar Association:

A friend of mine asked me how I rated coming to this great Association of learned lawyers to introduce the distinguished speaker. Well, I told him that when the news got out that the Bar Association was to have the pleasure of hearing the most distinguished lawyer of Great Britain, every member of the Bar Association asked Mr. Smith to let him have the honor of introducing him. Mr. Smith was in some trouble and gave an order that no man should have that honor except a lawyer whose record was one of perfect purity, who never had had a client and who had never charged any excessive fees, and that ruled out every member of the bar of North Carolina. So, as I was a licensed lawyer, it fell upon me to do the job because my record was perfect and pure, and it was so, because I never practiced law but one day and never had but one client.

But perhaps another reason was that Mr. Smith knew that in the World War one had the honor of directing the American Navy and that Navy and the British Navy cooperated so perfectly and harmoniously they drove the German U-boats off the face of the earth, and the sea, too.

And another reason was that I had known enough about Englishmen to know that all this stuff about their not taking a joke and enjoying them was bunk. As an example, when I was in London shortly after the World War during the Peace Conference, I found that the King of Britain had great humor. I lunched with him and he asked me this question, "I would like to ask you a question but if it embarrasses you, don't answer it." Very gracious in a king, I thought; they give orders. He said, "I don't understand, when you were in Washington and before you came over, you sent a very important and remarkable telegram to President Wilson in Paris." I said, "I don't know that I sent any very important telegram. I sent several cables." He said "The telegram you are said to have sent to President Wilson was 'Come home at once. If you don't, America will become a republic.' "

Ladies and Gentlemen, I have a much longer speech to make but I would be ashamed of myself if I kept you from the face before you. It is a great honor to welcome this distinguished gentleman to North Carolina. I am sure he feels that he is among friends and his own kindred; and here in particular in this section of North Carolina he is among the god-blessed Mc's sure as Britain is in the world. Ladies and Gentlemen, it is our pleasure tonight to hear the most distinguished lawyer in Britain, Sir Norman Birkett, whom I have the honor to present.

John C. Lewe presents

Thomas C. Clark

Thomas C. Clark, formerly Attorney General of the United States and Supreme Court justice was introduced at a meeting of the Executives' Club of Chicago by John C. Lewe, presiding justice of the Appellate Court of Illinois.

ONLY A FEW decades ago some facetious writer said that Texas was "the place where there are the most cows and the least milk, the most rivers and the least water in them, and where you can look the farthest and see the least." What he did not see was the enterprising and indomitable spirit of the Texans. Today, Texas is one of the great states of our union, ranking sixth in population and, to hear the Texans tell about it, it is first in every other respect.

Our speaker was born in Dallas forty-six years ago. He attended Virginia Military Institute and served with the 153rd Infantry in the first World War. Afterwards he studied at the University of Texas and was admitted to the Bar there in 1922. In a few short years, while associated with his father in the practice of law, he won an enviable place in the community. His fine talents and attainments had provided him with a lucrative law practice, but this he gave up in 1937 for an appointment as Special Attorney in the Department of Justice, Bureau of War Risk Litigation. He did not labor very long in obscurity. His sound common sense, his legal acumen and diligence in the discharge of his duties, were soon recognized in Washington. In 1940 he was made chief of the West Coast offices of the Anti-Trust Division. In 1942, he was appointed chief of the War Frauds Unit, and in 1943 Assistant Attorney General in charge of the Anti-Trust Division. He rose from the bottom level of the Department of Justice lawyers to attorney general of the nation in the short space of eight years. Though young in years and young in the point of service, in this exalted position he is boss of the biggest law office in the world.

Tom Clark is an earthy and homespun Texas lawyer with the smack and tang of elemental things — the rectitude and patience of the cliff. His subject is "The Attorney General and the Business Man."

I count it a high privilege to present to you the Attorney General of the United States.

THE MILITARY

Harry S. Truman presents
George C. Marshall

George Catlett Marshall (1880–1959) served as Chief of Staff of the United States Army during World War II. President Harry S. Truman, who succeeded to the presidency on the sudden death of Franklin D. Roosevelt (April 12, 1945), made the presentation to General Marshall of the Oak Leaf Cluster to Distinguished Service Medal, November 26, 1945, at the Pentagon.

IN A WAR unparalleled in magnitude and horror, millions of Americans gave their country outstanding service. General of the Army George C. Marshall gave it victory. By the favor of Providence, General Marshall became commander of the United States Army on the day that Germany attacked Poland. His was the vision that brought into being the strongest military force in history. Because he was able to make the Allies understand the true potentiality of American greatness in personnel and material, he was able to exercise greater influence than any other man on the strategy of victory. It was he who first recognized that victory in a global war would depend on this nation's capacity to ring the earth with far-flung supply lines, to arm every willing ally and to overcome the aggressor nations with superior firepower. He was the first to see the technological cunning and consequent greater danger of the Nazi enemy. He was the master proponent of a grand assault across the English Channel into Western Europe, directed by a single supreme allied commander. He insisted on maintaining unremitting pressure against the Japanese, thereby preventing them from becoming entrenched in their stolen empire and enabling our timely advances across the Pacific. He obtained from Congress the tremendous sums that made possible the atomic bomb, well knowing that failure would be his full responsibility. Statesman and soldier, he had cour-

141

age, fortitude and vision, and best of all, a rare self-effacement. He has been a tower of strength under two commanders-in-chief. His standards of character, conduct, and efficiency inspired the entire army, the nation and the world. To him, as much as to any individual, the United States owes its future. He takes his place at the head of the great commanders of history.

Francis Cardinal Spellman presents
Maxwell D. Taylor

At a state dinner given in his honor by the Lotos Club, January 27, 1966, General Maxwell D. Taylor received tributes from a number of the distinguished members and citizens present. Apparently unaware that he might be called upon to introduce the General, Francis Cardinal Spellman (1889–1967) responded quite spontaneously with wit and congeniality.

THIS COMES as a surprise to me. I didn't know I was going to be a speaker. However, I am delighted to be here and especially because of Max Taylor, of whom I am very proud to be a friend. I have been with him in many places where he has distinguished himself. As you can see, I have nothing prepared. I want to tell you, however, how I am responsible at least on one occasion for Max Taylor's going to Divine Service. It happened I had been very helpful in Korea: I had gotten food, clothing and medicine for Syngman Rhee, had collections and distributed them in Korea — there is no place where there is more need than in Korean orphanages — and so when I arrived on Christmas he had an arch made. I felt I was queen of the ball. There were inscriptions on it "Welcome Cardinal Spellman" and "Hail to Our Liberator, Our Protector."

In the Church, as well as in the Army, there is competition, and one of my competitors was greatly annoyed that there was no arch for him. I would have given him my arch, but there was no opportunity to do so. He sent back a telegram to the Department of Defense or the Secretary of War and wanted to know why I got all these honors in Korea. And the Secretary of the Army said General Taylor must be sure and go to church when my competitor was speaking on Christmas Day. So the incident ended happily because General Taylor showed up with his staff and a few Catholics with him.

So my competitor had enough for Christmas and that night was back in Los Angeles. And I am glad I did such a good work in getting General Taylor to go to Divine Service. I might have gotten him myself if I hadn't gotten the arch. I did not prepare a speech, and I do not have adjectives to describe General Taylor. He is a great person, a wonderful American, an outstanding general, and now comes his latest honor, a member of the Lotos Club.

George Wharton Pepper presents
Ferdinand Foch

At the banquet tendered Ferdinand Foch, World War I Marshal of France, by the citizens of Philadelphia, at the Bellevue-Stratford Hotel, November 15, 1921, the presiding officer, the distinguished lawyer Senator George Wharton Pepper, said:

THIS OCCASION will live forever in the memory of everybody in this room except our guest. To him this is merely another gathering of Americans eager to do him honor. You and I, however, are sharing an experience which we have coveted all our lives.

How often have we wished that it could have been our good fortune to get even a glimpse of the great ones of history! When I was a boy I longed for a sight of those old-time heroes, Aetius and Theodoric, who overcame Attila the Hun at Châlons-sur-Marne. What an inspiration it would have been to see Charles Martel, who, at the battle of Tours, saved the liberties and religion of Europe. How often we have wished that we could feel the spell which would have been cast upon us in the presence of Charlemagne or of Jeanne d'Arc, or of the great Condé. What would we not give for a reminiscence of the first Napoleon, or of our own Washington? But tonight, my friends, the aspirations of a lifetime are more than realized. We are not only in the presence of one whom History will forever cherish in the inner shrine of her Temple of Fame, but we are actually standing in the intimate relation to him of hosts to a beloved guest.

He will surely pardon us if we speak of him for a moment as if he were not within earshot. Only thus can we assure ourselves that we are awake and not mere wanderers in a land of radiant dreams.

Here — in our midst — is the man who in August of 1914 successfully defended the line of the Meurthe when the numerical odds against him were as ten is to one. Here before our very eyes is the leader upon whom Joffre wisely staked his all at the first battle of the Marne — the man who, at the center of the line, and with only 70,000 men behind him, attacked with the audacity of genius the 300,000 marshaled against him by von Bülow and von Hausen. Here is the commander who, as he watched the seventh charge of the theretofore invincible Prussian Guard, remarked cheerfully, and with unerring instinct, to his staff: "Well, gentlemen, they must be in great straits somewhere or other if they are in such a desperate hurry here!" Here the intrepid leader who, when the Germans pierced his line at La Fère Champenoise, refused to concede it, and though he had no reserves of any kind left, withdrew a division from the line, risking a gap, and stormed La Fère just as the Germans were sitting down at dinner, thinking the battle was over and won! Here is the man to whom, when the fall of Antwerp was imminent, Joffre again turned as the only soldier who could preserve the left flank of the Allies from destruction. With your own eyes you are beholding the strategist whose comprehension of the German military mind was thereafter well-nigh ignored for three terrible years until the war was lost, and he was given supreme command with instructions to win it. You are looking into the flashing eyes of the patriot who entirely disregarded himself in accepting the greatest responsibility which has ever devolved upon the shoulders of one man — the inspired genius who, within six months thereafter, having turned defeat into victory, was thundering at the Hindenburg line and driving the enemy to that certain destruction from which they were saved only by unconditional surrender.

This is the man who declares, Victory resides in will — the unconquerable spirit which affirms that a battle won is a battle in which one has not admitted one's defeat. This is the benefactor of the world, who, by a paradox of history, has with force of arms made possible the conditions in which we may seriously consider the limitation of armaments. This is that gentleman of France who, by graciously accepting the hospitality of the American Legion, shows himself willing to be reckoned the brother-in-arms of every American soldier. This is that simple-hearted and humble-minded man of

God whom we rightly regard as the protector of every American home.

It is not for me — or for anyone — to present this man. Men and women of Philadelphia, I call upon you to rise in place and give expression to the everlasting gratitude which you feel to M. Ferdinand Foch, Maréchal de France.

Samuel L. Clemens *presents*

Joseph B. Hawley

General Joseph B. Hawley, United States Senator from Connecticut, 1881–1905, addressed a Republican meeting at Elmira, New York, in 1881, where he was introduced by Samuel L. Clemens. The introduction is reprinted by permission of copyright owners from *Mark Twain: A Biography*, by Albert Bigelow Paine. Copyright 1912, by Harper and Brothers; copyright 1940, by Dora L. Paine.

I SEE I am advertised to introduce the speaker of the evening . . . and I see it is the report that I am to make a political speech. Now, I must say this is an error. I wasn't constructed to make stump speeches. . . . General Hawley was President of the Centennial Commission. He was a gallant soldier in the war. He has been Governor of Connecticut, member of Congress, and was President of the convention that nominated Abraham Lincoln —

General Hawley: "That nominated Grant."

He says it was Grant, but I know better. He is a member of my church at Hartford and the author of "Beautiful Snow." Maybe he will deny that. But I am only here to give him a character from his last place. As a pure citizen, I respect him; as a personal friend of years, I have the warmest regard for him; as a neighbor whose vegetable garden adjoins mine, why — why, I watch him. That's nothing; we all do that with any neighbor. General Hawley keeps his promises not only in private but in public. . . . He is broad-souled, generous, noble, liberal, alive to his moral and religious responsibilities. Whenever the contribution box was passed I never knew him to take out a cent. He is a square, true, honest man in politics, and I must say he occupies a mighty lonesome position. . . . He is an American of Americans. Would we had more such men! So broad, so bountiful is his character that he never turned a tramp empty-handed from his door, but always gave him a letter of introduction to me. . . . Pure, honest, incorruptible, that is Joe Hawley. Such a man in politics is like a bottle of perfumery in a glue factory — it may modify the stench if it doesn't destroy it. And now, in speaking thus highly of the speaker of the evening, I haven't said any more of him than I would say of myself. Ladies and Gentlemen, this is General Hawley.

Charles T. Fisher Jr. presents
George C. Kenney

At the June 5, 1950, meeting of the Economic Club of Detroit, General George C. Kenney was the principal speaker. He was introduced by the presiding officer, Charles T. Fisher, Jr., president of the National Bank of Detroit.

OUR GUEST of honor today, the Commanding General, Air University, United States Air Force, was a combat pilot in World War I, and Chief of the Pacific Air Command in World War II. General Douglas MacArthur said, in describing him during the Pacific war, "General Kenney is unquestionably one of the best qualified air officers in the world today." At the same time he was being called a "soldiers' general" by "his kids," the officers and enlisted men of his command, whose admiration and respect he won immediately. A third appraisal was that of a "most unorthodox Commander," a title of acclaim accorded him by appreciative correspondents and military analysts attached to his headquarters.

In those three estimates lie the qualities and characteristics that raised our speaker from a first lieutenant to a four-star general in the years between the First and the close of the Second World War. They embody his dynamic energy, his imaginative yet efficient approach to baffling problems, and his ability to inspire men. Those, coupled with his professional knowledge gained as a pilot and engineer expert, produced the unorthodox tactics which turned the tide of the battle of the Pacific.

He introduced skip-bombing, lob-bombing, and a special bomb fuse which made the Nipponese Navy a duck hunt for his Air Force. He scrapped the technical manuals and mounted eight, and later twelve, .50 caliber guns in the fuselage and nose of his B-25 Mitchells, and six in the A-20 Bostons, making them the terrors of the Pacific. He invented the destructive parachute bomb and produced countless other bomb improvisations, until they, in his own words, "sang all the notes in the scale; cut through the trees two inches thick and a hundred feet away, like a knife; and when they landed in the jungle, slashed enough room for a baseball diamond."

He drove his men to perform miraculous deeds with limited equipment, while he pressed Washington for more planes, in the early days of the war. And at all times he enjoyed this great opportunity to prove in fact the doctrine that he had been preaching since Billy Mitchell's day, that air power was the beginning and end of modern martial movement, and a primary weapon of decision in warfare.

Our guest's biography appeared in some detail in the announcement of this meeting; therefore, it is unnecessary for me to review it.

Gentlemen, it is my privilege and great pleasure to introduce to you our speaker, General George Churchill Kenney.

RELIGION AND

SOCIAL WORK

Arthur B. Langlie presents
Norman S. Marshall

Commissioner Norman S. Marshall, who retired as national commander of the Salvation Army in 1963, was the guest of honor at the Newcomen dinner in New York, February 18, 1960. He was introduced by Arthur B. Langlie, then president of the McCall Corporation.

IT IS SAID that a "friend" is one who is coming in the door when everyone else is leaving, and that "success" in life is achievement in serving your fellow man, with or without profit, that brings a maximum of satisfaction to the individual rendering the service.

Our speaker tonight qualifies both as a "friend," and as a "success."

He is my friend, he is yours. In fact, he is qualified as a friend of man everywhere, for directly or indirectly he is always coming in to help the individual in trouble whenever poverty, sickness, confusion and utter despair confronts him.

He began his successful career as a boy of ten. Both of his parents were Salvation Army pioneers, and three of his four brothers and his only sister became Salvation Army officers.

Through the years, Norman Marshall has had most of the vital experiences in life that make Salvationists such wonderful people.

He entered training for officership in the Salvation Army in Chicago in 1914. After being commissioned, he filled various positions in the Dakotas and from there he began serving in locations all over the United States. He has had much to do in the training programs of Salvation Army youth. He was made the National Commander of the Salvation Army in September 1957.

Commissioner Marshall is a member of numerous national and international organizations devoted to helping people. He is also a past director of the New York Rotary Club; a member of the New

York Chapter of the Military Order of World Wars; and now a member of the Newcomen Society in North America.

Commissioner Marshall was married in 1917. His wife was a captain in the Salvation Army and has ably supported him in their joint work. They have four children, and carrying on the family tradition two of them have become Salvation Army officers.

It is a great privilege to present to you a friend to all of us, one whose success story shouts from the housetops the virtues of a free society, and whose career personifies man's opportunities therein to supplant degradation, despair and frustration, with love and hope and faith: Commissioner Norman S. Marshall.

William T. Gossett presents
Harry Emerson Fosdick

The eminent pastor emeritus of the Riverside Church, New York, Harry Emerson Fosdick, spoke to the Economic Club of Detroit, May 19, 1952, and was introduced by William T. Gossett, vice president and general counsel of the Ford Motor Company and a former president of the board of trustees of the Riverside Church of New York City.

SOME TWENTY-SEVEN years ago I went to New York to enter Columbia Law School. I was under strict injunction from my mother to go to hear a minister named Harry Emerson Fosdick, whose sermons she had heard over the radio. "Well," I said, "just another minister, I suppose," but I nevertheless went to the Park Avenue Baptist Church where he was then preaching. I did not see Dr. Fosdick at all. With hundreds of others I heard his sermon amplified as part of a separate service in the basement of the church. That did not discourage me in the slightest because on that and on succeeding Sundays I was thrilled and inspired by one brilliant sermon after another.

Here was an exponent of a liberal, dynamic, and vital religion, free of much of the dogma which had seemed so intellectually unpalatable to me.

It was not long afterwards that the people of his congregation built for Dr. Fosdick a larger church, the now famous Riverside Church, on Riverside Drive in New York. But still there was an overflow. With a sanctuary built to seat 2,500, there were sometimes as many as 4,000 in the congregation. Here obviously was a man with something to say; something of importance and value to a great many people. There was no secret key to his appeal, and no blatant evangelism of a sort designed to attract crowds. Instead there was always a well-reasoned and penetrating message, and behind it a sincere and all-pervading purpose.

157

This was a man who sought even as a youth to see Christian truth in relationship to all the rest of man's knowledge; who claimed his Christian liberty to rethink the Gospel in the light of new knowledge; and who gloried in the task of helping to open wide the doors of Christian faith for men of many races and many sects.

In his own words, "Christian faith flows from one generation's way of thinking to another; out of prescientific ages into knowledge; out of monarchy and feudalism into democracy. And the only way to keep it is to move with it, rethinking the meaning of Christianity's eternal verities as the days come."

From the pulpit he preached the Gospel of God's love and man's duty, always with a deep understanding of human needs, with impelling power and with utter fearlessness. Once he told his congregation this: "Always the understanding between us has been clear: that we do not have to agree, but that you want in the pulpit a preacher upon whom you can count to say what he honest to goodness thinks."

It was inevitable that the inspiring thoughts and words of this man of God should go far beyond the confines of the immediate church. Over a period of years millions of Americans have come to know him through his books and other writings. These have been translated into many languages, and millions of copies have been sold all over the world. His radio sermons over a network of 125 stations reached each Sunday an estimated audience of 25 million people in this country, and millions abroad who heard him over short wave. His was the good voice of America. It is not surprising therefore that he has been called one of the great religious leaders of all times.

Just six years ago this week, after more than forty years in the ministry (almost sixteen of them as Pastor of the Riverside Church), Dr. Fosdick insisted upon retiring to the well-earned post of Pastor Emeritus. I had the honor of representing the Board of Trustees of the church at what will always remain in my memory as one of the finest farewell tributes any minister could receive from his flock. By that time the Riverside Church had become one of the great religious institutions of the nation. One of its most unique characteristics attributable to Dr. Fosdick is that affirmation of faith in Christ is the only requirement for membership, with baptism in any form requested, or without baptism. All Christians, regardless of denominational background, are eligible for membership. . . .

Few ministers of the Gospel can look back over accomplishments comparable to those which I have so briefly and inadequately described. But I am sure that what comes closest to Dr. Fosdick's heart is the realization that his life has had such a profound influence upon the lives of so many millions of others.

In these perilous times we need inspired guidance. I know of no man in America who is better qualified to point out to us those eternal truths which many of us feel must be faced if we are to find a way out of the complexities of our times. It is an honor and a privilege to present him to you today. My friends, Dr. Fosdick.

W. O. DuVall presents
Billy Graham

The world-renowned minister of the gospel received the Great American Award in Atlanta December 29, 1967. On this occasion he was introduced to an audience of business, civic, and religious leaders of the city by Colonel W. O. DuVall, chairman of the board of the Atlanta Federal Savings and Loan Association.

THE HONOR of presenting to you Dr. Billy Graham is a distinct privilege. It is with pride in his accomplishments that we recognize his greatness.

His career is distinguished by his dedication to the highest ideals of the Christian ministry. The Graham tradition of service, humility, and leadership is already indelibly written in the history of our time for all posterity to honor and to cherish.

Dr. Graham was born in our neighboring state of North Carolina. His early boyhood was spent in North and South Carolina, but he moved to Florida to begin his higher education. There he received the Bachelor of Theology degree from the Florida Bible Institute in 1940 and in the same year was ordained as a Baptist minister. From Florida he moved on to Wheaton College where he received a Bachelor of Arts degree in 1943. Indeed, 1943 was an important year in the young minister's life. While attending Wheaton College he met, wooed, and won the charming Ruth McCue Bell, one of his undergraduate classmates. From this union, there are five children, Virginia, Anne, Ruth, Franklin, and Nelson. Two of the daughters are now happily married and have presented the Grahams with two fine grandchildren.

The life of Mrs. Graham has been so full and fruitful that I must pay tribute to her and express appreciation for her influence on the man whom we honor this evening. She was born in China, the daughter of Dr. and Mrs. Nelson Bell, Presbyterian medical missionaries, whose family has given to the Presbyterian church and our Christian society many dedicated servants of God.

Mrs. Graham has maintained the Graham home at Montreat, North Carolina, raised the family, and "kept the home fires burning," while her famous husband carried the message of Christ to the ends of the earth. It was also in 1943 that Billy Graham became the pastor of his first church at Western Springs, Illinois, as well as beginning his great radio ministry over station WCFL, Chicago, with his presentation of "Songs in the Night." From this beginning, almost a quarter century ago, Billy Graham has become the greatest radio and television evangelist of all times, carrying a message of light and hope to the people of every nation.

While serving as President of the Northwestern College in Minneapolis in 1950, he founded the Billy Graham Evangelistic Association and began his weekly radio program "The Hour of Decision."

Today, this program is carried into every home in America and around the world by radio and television. People in foreign lands may not know our leading diplomats and may not even know much about Lyndon Johnson, but everywhere the name of Billy Graham is known, honored, and respected.

Dr. Graham is the author of many books that mean so much to so many people and currently writes the syndicated column "My Answer" which is carried in 146 daily newspapers throughout our country. Some of his better known works are *Peace with God, The Secret of Happiness,* and *World Aflame.*

Dr. Graham has received so many awards and honorary degrees that time will not allow me to catalog them. He is a member of the Royal Geographic Society, the Royal Literary Society, received the Freedoms Foundation Award for Distinguished Persons, the Gold Award of the George Washington Carver Memorial Institute, the Golden Plate Award from the American Academy of Achievement, and was named one of the "Ten Most Admired Men in the World." Just this year, he received the Silver Medallion from the National Conference of Christians and Jews.

Dr. Graham has led crusades in almost every nation of the world and has preached, face to face, to more than 75 million people. Through these crusades, together with his radio and television services, he has touched the lives of more people in the name of Christ than any man in the history of Christianity.

His service to humanity cuts across all denominational, social, and racial lines, and brings a message of love and joy to all people. Truly we are privileged this evening to sit at the feet of greatness and to recognize and honor him for his life of service and dedication.

Dr. Billy Graham.

Walter Croarkin presents
William David O'Brien

Msgr. Croarkin, pastor of St. Agnes Church, Chicago Heights, Illinois, introduced Archbishop O'Brien (1878–1962), president of the Catholic Church Extension Society, shortly after the Archbishop celebrated his Golden Jubilee as a priest in November 1953.

ARCHBISHOP O'BRIEN recently celebrated his Golden Jubilee as a priest, at which time he was elevated to the dignity of Archbishop. A few Sundays ago hundreds of ecclesiastics of all ranks and people from all walks of life assembled at the Cathedral in Chicago to honor him in one of the greatest outpourings of admiration and affection ever tendered to a bishop. I should like to think that his presence with us this morning, so soon after that celebration, is a continuation of the ceremony, an opportunity for the people of this community to rejoice with him and thank God for him.

Archbishop O'Brien has given the major part of his years and talents to the Catholic Church Extension Society of America. As the title indicates, this Society extends the scope and influence of the Church to remote and impoverished places all over America. For the noble work of the Extension Society, Archbishop O'Brien has been untiring in his energy and he has been shameless in his efforts to provide funds for that great work. Indeed, Archbishop O'Brien calls himself the beggar, but because his begging has been only a means to an end, his real title should not be a "beggar" but the bestower, the giver, the benefactor. I am thinking first of all of the priests and sisters and people throughout our American mission lands who thank God daily that this great beggar has so unselfishly and successfully begged for them. But today I am conscious of his amazing solicitude for me personally, his fatherly interest and kindness manifested in so many ways that I am truly flabbergasted.

Your Excellency, you have done a wonderful thing for the great Archdiocese of Chicago. Your friends rave and rightly so about the tangible things you have done for the Church of Christ, which you love so well, but I respectfully suggest that some of your greatest contributions to the Church have been the intangibles — your human quality, that delightfully common touch, that heavenly humor, that great heart, which you have always shown us. In the warmth of your personality, your fellow men, especially your fellow priests, in your home diocese, have been melted into a happy and harmonious fusion. Archbishop O'Brien has learned what only truly great men have discovered, that in coming down to the level of the ordinary man, he has been lifted to a pedestal, that the more he humbled himself, the more we exalt him. In my memory of thirty years in the priesthood, I have never known of a bishop so universally admired and loved as Archbishop O'Brien.

Archbishop O'Brien is titular Archbishop of Calinda. I am told that nobody knows exactly where Calinda is, that this archdiocese has been lost in the shadows of history, but, Your Excellency, may I respectfully submit that I know where your archdiocese is. It is in the hearts of the many lonely and discouraged priests that you have helped in the mission fields. It is in the hearts of the thousands of men and women and children who, because of your zeal, have enjoyed the consolations of our Holy Faith. It is in the hearts of the priests of this great archdiocese who have achieved an incomparable *esprit de corps*, because of your genial, fatherly, and priestly contact with us. Your Excellency, that is where your archdiocese is and, if I were you, I wouldn't trade it for any other archdiocese in the whole wide world.

Walter Croarkin presents

Frank F. Rosenthal

In 1967, Rabbi Rosenthal, spiritual leader and chief rabbi of the congregation of Temple Anshe Sholom, was introduced by Msgr. Croarkin, pastor of St. Agnes Church, Chicago Heights, Illinois, and chairman of the South Suburban Inter-Faith Clergy and Lay Council.

ONCE UPON A TIME – to be precise ten years ago – there was a group of people who wanted to be truly God's people. They had a tradition that indicated such was their divine mission. Long ago God had called them to the sublime vocation of spiritual leadership. In a world deluded, misled, debased by false gods, they were to proclaim and bear witness to the fact that there is indeed a God, not a God made by man but a pure spirit Who has repeatedly manifested His many wonderful attributes, especially His love.

In spite of His transcendent qualities this God is a Person, more so than any other person who only analogically can claim to be like Him. Because He is the person par excellence His relationship with His chosen people would be the most personal relationship imaginable. No other person could, like Him, be as tender, appealing, jealous, hurt, angry, forgiving, loving. The account of what has happened between this Person Who is most a Person and these people who in so many ways are most a people is the most interesting, dramatic story on record.

Through the centuries it has unfolded, page after page, an inspiring, poignant, triumphant high romance. A recent and local chapter has been written right here in this part of God's beautiful world. It is found in the annals of Temple Anshe Sholom, a notable group of God's people who came together, united by their noble spiritual heritage, and eager to go forward with their divine mandate, to relate to the place and the time in which they lived, to witness to the

165

one true God, and to make Him a vital force in the community where His Providence had placed them.

They were a people, blessed by God with many talents, eager to be the yeast, the ferment, the little bit of leaven that would lift men up to God. But as in all times and all places they needed someone who would make their thoughts articulate, their light radiant, their warmth felt. They needed a Moses who would lead them out of the Egypt of their frustrations and restrictions to the Promised Land of fulfillment, a Joshua who would make unfriendly walls come tumbling down, a David, "a man after God's own heart," who would unify them and establish a new Jerusalem, a modern city of God.

That they found such a man is our joyous reason for being here tonight. For the last ten years this congregation, under his wise and warm guidance, has risen to a position of spiritual, intellectual, and social influence that has blessed all our community.

Tonto often referred to the Lone Ranger with admiration and affection in the words Kee-me-sah-bee, which in his Indian language meant "faithful friend." It should be a source of deep satisfaction for one man to hear from another man the statement: He has never let me down. This I can say about Rabbi Rosenthal. To me he has always been Kee-me-sah-bee, my faithful friend.

But I think I should welcome a chance to speak about him for more than what he has meant to me personally. I should like to speak for many others. As pastor of the two thousand families that make up St. Agnes Parish, as Chairman of the South Suburban Inter-Faith Clergy and Lay Council, in the name of the Ministerial Association of Chicago Heights and Homewood-Flossmoor, as one who has lived intimately with this community for twenty-five years and is therefore somewhat qualified to know what it thinks and what it feels, I gladly, eagerly, seize this opportunity to acknowledge publicly the outstanding leadership of Rabbi Rosenthal and the equally outstanding followership of the members of Temple Anshe Sholom. There is a popular song that says, "You can't have one without the other." So it has been with this Temple and this Rabbi.

On ancient Italian sundials there were often inscribed words which said: "For every hour that passes, a memory. For every hour that tarries, a happiness. For every hour that comes, a hope."

The last ten years have deposited in the Bank of Eternity, where they can never be destroyed, tender and marvelous memories. The present hour that tarries with us is an hour of happiness that is well deserved and should be relished. And for the hours yet to come there is indeed hope that Rabbi Rosenthal and Temple Anshe Sholom will recognize their rendezvous with a bright future, their vocation, their genius, to be a revelation of the goodness, and beauty, and love of God.

SCIENCE AND

ENGINEERING

Warren Weaver presents
Sir Charles Percy Snow

Sir Charles Percy Snow, later Baron Snow of Leicester, the British novelist and physicist, acquired international fame with the publication of
The Two Cultures (the Rede lecture, 1959) in which he dealt with the
inability of men of science to communicate with those in the humanities.
Long associated with Cambridge University, he was presented at the
1960 annual meeting of the American Association for the Advancement
of Science by Dr. Warren Weaver of the Alfred P. Sloan Foundation.

WE LIVE, as our grandparents did not, in a highly interconnected
world.

The political, geographic, and communicative interconnections
are made almost painfully obvious every morning when we listen
to the radio news. Laos and Leopoldville, Moscow and Manila,
Johannesburg and Jakarta are with us at the breakfast table, as immediate and pressing as the signal for the school bus. And across our
evening sky there swims a communication satellite, symbol of the fact
that both voice and vision can now extend over our whole planet.

Even more significant, however, are the new interconnections
which are developing within the world of the mind. There used to
be comforting compartments within any one of which a person could
live and work and think, reasonably protected against — almost in-
sulated from — the rest of the world of ideas. But, largely in the last
half century, this has ceased to be so.

This vanishing of intellectual boundaries has, in particular, occurred inside science. About 1920 the line between chemistry and
physics began to disappear. At superficial levels of application —
the cookery level of chemistry and the hardware level of physics —
one can still tell the two subjects apart. But fundamentally they
have now become one.

171

Even more spectacular and surprising is the fact that biology is now in the process of becoming completely absorbed into and merged with all the rest of science. The modern molecular biologist is a chemist, a physicist, a mathematician, a submicroscopic cytologist — in short, a *scientist*. The origin of the elements, the origin of life, and the origin of species — these have now become interrelated parts of one grand problem.

In the good old days when chemistry still smelled like chemistry and biology stayed put inside the biology building, when physics was the harmless preoccupation of a few professors, when mathematics consisted of one useful part called arithmetic and a second part that any sensible person recognized as incomprehensible — in those good old days our grandfathers really did not have cause for much general worry or concern about science. One was relatively free to take it or leave it alone. Electric motors and lights and automobiles and better medicines and some improved seeds were becoming available, and that all seemed a good idea. A very few persons were confused and troubled about what they supposed science had to say about religion. The poets occasionally sneered at science, but this was pretty well canceled out by the fact that scientists kept on reading poetry.

Although there were a few prophets, the vast proportion of men knew little or nothing about science and did not — at least consciously or obviously — suffer from that fact.

This has now all been changed. We now realize that science cannot be disregarded. We now know that science is intertwined not only with political and economic problems but with all the concerns of the humanists and artists. We now know that the mind and spirit of man approaches reality from many directions, appreciates order and beauty in many manifestations, and by joining all forces brings creative imagination and revealing insight to bear on all aspects of nature, of life, and of living. We now know that the poet and the physicist, the musician and the mathematician, the artist and the statesman, and the philosopher and the astronomer attack their problems with essentially the same intellectual and spiritual resources.

But although everyone realizes that our geographical world has become one and that the political world is intimately interrelated, most men are more tardy, or more reluctant, to recognize and profit by the emerging unity of the world of the mind.

Sir Charles Percy Snow has become recognized as the most authoritative and most moving spokesman for the view that we must rejoin the pieces of our fractured culture, must restore the unity of the world of the mind. Himself a distinguished practitioner in science and in the creative arts, he has made a responsible and reasoned plea that our culture be a unified one.

He speaks to us on a theme which deals with one of the most interesting and difficult aspects of the interrelatedness of science with all the rest of life, an interrelationship which many disregard, which most debate, and which some deny — the moral unneutrality of science.

G. Lynn Sumner presents

Victor Heiser

Dr. Victor Heiser, an expert on tropical diseases and their prevention, published his autobiography, *An American Doctor's Odyssey*, in 1936. Reprinted by the permission of the publishers from *We Have With Us Tonight* by G. Lynn Sumner. Copyrighted in 1941 by Harper & Row, Publishers, Inc.

ON A DARK May day in 1889, a boy saw his father and mother swept to their death in the torrent and terror of the Johnstown flood. He could not save them, but the miracle of his own survival has meant the saving of literally millions of other lives in every corner of the world.

He became a great doctor, but he was impatient with the comparative futility of healing one body at a time. He wanted to strike at the great scourges of the earth, the devastating diseases that attack nations and races. Recognition in high places of his skill and understanding and wisdom has made all that possible. First in the United States Immigration Department, then for ten years as Health Commissioner of the Philippines, then for twenty years as Director for the East of the International Health Board of the Rockefeller Foundation, Dr. Heiser has devoted himself to stamping out disease wherever helpless peoples suffer in the world. Of his own achievements, he has said: "Nothing in my life has given me such joy as to see the light of hope slowly kindled in faces once set in lines of despair."

In 1934 he retired to write the story of this great adventure in physical salvation. That book, *An American Doctor's Odyssey*, is a classic that should be required reading for every American.

Dr. Heiser is assuredly one of the most interesting men in all the world. He could, if he would, tell you tales of breathless, fascinating interest. For example, of the awful moment when on his quick decision rested the life of a future king of England. He could tell you how later he conspired with that same Prince of Wales to change the style of evening dress for Englishmen in India. And he could tell you how he walked the streets of hostile Tokyo, guarded by ghosts, when the hands of strangers would suddenly appear to light his cigarettes. But whatever he may say, it is a great privilege to present a great doctor, a great humanitarian, a great American — Dr. Victor Heiser.

Louis Nizer presents
Albert Einstein

Einstein (1879–1955), Nobel Prize winner of 1922, is best known as the discoverer and exponent of the theory of relativity. He was appointed a life member of the Institute for Advanced Study, Princeton, in 1933. The following introduction is by Louis Nizer, prominent New York attorney.

IT IS SAID of a mythological Greek hero that by extraordinary physical skill he was able to jump from the surface of the earth to the planets and, after accumulating the wisdom of his visits, return to the earth to be worshipped as a god for his superior knowledge.

In recent years a great scientist among us has been able, not by virtue of great physical strength but by virtue of a penetrating mind, to lift himself from the surface of the earth and explore the mysteries of the universe. We revere him; yes, almost worship him as one of the great men of the ages.

From one dark little corner of this world he has been exiled. Sometimes I doubt that Einstein and Reinhardt and Thomas Mann have been exiled from Germany. Rather I think Germany is in exile from them.

When I think of that blacked-out region of the earth, I believe it is sacrilegious to say that man was made in the image of God. But when I think of Professor Einstein, I know it is devout to believe that man was made in the image of God. He, more than any other man of the past few centuries, is destined to immortality.

Ladies and Gentlemen — Professor Albert Einstein.

Juan T. Trippe presents
Vannevar Bush

More than any other man of his time, Vannevar Bush was concerned with the management of large-scale scientific research during World War II. He served as president of the Carnegie Institution of Washington from 1939 to 1955. He spoke before the Economic Club of New York, November 15, 1950, and was presented by Juan T. Trippe, president of the club and president of Pan American Airways.

OUR FIRST speaker tonight, Dr. Vannevar Bush, is a great scientist and a great administrator. His varied career began with General Electric in 1913; then to Tufts College; to Massachusetts Institute of Technology; and finally to Carnegie Institution of Washington, where he has been president since 1939.

During World War I he was engaged in research on submarine detection for the United States Navy. Even before this country entered World War II, he put his great talents at the service of this nation. Under his direction as chief of the Office of Scientific Research and Development, many of the great weapons that won World War II were developed. Those weapons revolutionized warfare on land, on sea and in the air. They came into our hands just in time to tip the scales of victory in favor of our armies, our fleets, and our airmen throughout the world.

The proximity fuse is one example. In the Pacific our fleets, including even powerful Task Force 58, were sorely pressed by Japanese suicide pilots. These kamikazes hurled their aircraft, as humanly-guided missiles, into our naval vessels with appalling effectiveness. Into that unequal struggle we threw the proximity fuse, and the proximity fuse saved the day for our arms. The armadas of MacArthur and Nimitz sailed on to victory.

Radar is another of the World War II weapons whose usefulness was greatly improved under Dr. Bush's leadership. Also under his direction the atomic bomb was brought from the theoretical stage and placed into the hands of our military forces as a practical weapon. Not only was the atomic bomb a decisive factor in bringing the Pacific war to a favorable conclusion, but since V-J Day it has prevented the conquest of Western Europe and the free world by the hordes of Soviet Russia. Though today's peace is an uneasy one, we can credit to our possession of the atomic bomb such borrowed time as the free nations have in which to redress the balance of power.

Dr. Bush's accomplishments have their roots not only in a deep and intimate knowledge of science but also in an understanding of men, in an iron will, and in a subtle judgment as to how to deal with overwhelming problems.

Winston Churchill said of the gallant Royal Air Force after the Air Battle of Britain ten years ago: "Never in the history of recorded events have so many owed so much to so few." Tonight, if Mr. Churchill were with us, I believe he and all of us could properly say: "Never in the history of recorded events have the free peoples of the world owed so much to a single man."

Dr. Vannevar Bush's subject this evening is "The Sinews of Peace." Because he is one of the most distinguished scientists of this generation, it is an honor, and because he is my friend, it is a pleasure to present him to this audience.

Warren G. Harding presents
Marie S. Curie

Madame Marie Curie (1867–1934), eminent scientist and co-discoverer with her husband, Pierre Curie, of radium in 1898, arrived in Washington, May 20, 1921, to receive from the hands of the President of the United States a gram of radium presented to her by the women of America. In presenting the gift to Madame Curie, Warren G. Harding, twenty-eighth President of the United States, said in part:

WE GREET you as foremost among scientists in the age of science, as leader among women in the generation which sees woman come tardily into her own. We greet you as an exemplar of liberty's victories in the generation wherein liberty has won her crown of glory.

In doing honor to you we testify anew our pride in the ancient friendships which have bound us to both the country of your adoption and that of your nativity. We exalt anew our pride that we have stood with them in the struggle for civilization and have touched elbows with them in the march of progress.

It has been your fortune, Madame Curie, to accomplish an immortal work for humanity. We are not without understanding of the trials and sacrifices which have been the price of your achievement. We know something of the fervid purpose and deep devotion which inspired you. We bring to you the meed of honor which is due pre-eminence in science, scholarship, research, and humanitarianism. But with it all we bring something more. We lay at your feet the testimony of that love which all the generations of men have been wont to bestow upon the noble woman, the unselfish wife, the devoted mother.

In testimony of the affection of the American people, of their confidence in your scientific work, and of their earnest wish that your genius and energy may receive all encouragement to carry forward your efforts for the advance of science and the conquest of disease, I have been commissioned to present to you this little phial of radium. To you we owe our knowledge and possession of it, and so to you we give it, confident that in your possession it will be the means further to unveil the fascinating secrets of nature, to widen the field of useful knowledge, to alleviate suffering among the children of men. Take it to use as your wisdom shall direct and your purpose of service shall incline you. Be sure that we esteem it but a small earnest of the sentiments for which it stands. It betokens the affection of one great people for another. It will remind you of the love of a grateful people for yourself; and it will testify, in the useful work to which you will devote it, to the reverence of mankind for one of its foremost benefactors and most beloved women.

Thomas W. Martin presents
Charles F. Kettering

Charles F. Kettering (1876–1958), long-time head of General Motors' research division, was renowned as an inventor and scientist. At the third annual dinner meeting of the Southern Research Institute, November 12, 1947, he was introduced by Thomas W. Martin, chairman of the board of the Alabama Power Company, Birmingham.

IT IS NOW my privilege to present the speaker of the evening.

Recently a friend sent me from General Motors what was called a thumbnail sketch of Dr. Kettering — but it is sixteen typed pages; and every line is interesting and thrilling. Most of us know that he is responsible for more inventions that touch our personal and business lives than any man in American life for the past fifty years; indeed, one writer recently extended that period to embrace the whole life of the Republic.

One of the far-reaching activities to which Dr. Kettering has pledged support is the Sloan-Kettering Institute for Cancer Research, announced August 8, 1945, in which he and Mr. Alfred P. Sloan, Jr., Chairman of General Motors, linked themselves as co-sponsors and active trustees.

Dr. Kettering was born on a farm near Loudonville, Ohio. He is a graduate of Ohio State University; belongs to thirty-two scientific and educational organizations (or did until he came to Birmingham); possesses twenty honorary degrees from American colleges; and at least fourteen other honors have been conferred upon him by universities, scientific and other societies.

Announcement was made in June last of his retirement. However, a southern newspaper said at the time: "We'll believe Boss Kettering has retired when the last mystery of the universe has been solved; and even then Ket would be off to find a new universe." That statement, Dr. Kettering, sums up the confidence and the respect we people of the South have for you.

A very human person, Dr. Kettering likes people and gets along well with individuals of any rank. Among those who work for him and with him, he is affectionately known as "Boss Ket."

It is a great privilege now to present Dr. Charles Franklin Kettering, until recently vice president and director of General Motors Corporation and general manager of General Motors Research Laboratories, one of America's most distinguished scientists and industrialists.

William R. Willcox presents
George W. Goethals

George W. Goethals (1858–1928) was appointed by President Theodore Roosevelt in 1907 as chief engineer of the Panama Canal after two civilian engineers had resigned. He carried the work to completion. He was guest speaker at the twenty-seventh dinner meeting of the Economic Club of New York, March 5, 1914, and was introduced on this occasion by William R. Willcox, vice-president of the Club.

FELLOW MEMBERS of the Economic Club, Friends, and Guests: I am extremely sorry that our president, Mr. Speyer, is not with us this evening, but I esteem it an unusual privilege to preside on this occasion, when our dinner is given in honor of so distinguished a guest as Colonel Goethals. No enterprise of modern times, whether public or private has, because of its very great importance, received so much attention from the civilized world as has the completing of the Panama Canal. No other enterprise has called for so large an outlay of money, and while other engineering problems, difficult and as complex as those at Panama, have been met and solved, there has been none of such large and commanding magnitude. For many years it has been the dream of our legislators that the Canal should be built across the Isthmus of Panama, or across the contiguous territory thereto, in order that the commerce of our country might be relieved of the long trip around the Horn, and also to bring our country into closer shipping relations with the lands of the Pacific. It remained, however, for President Roosevelt to turn this dream of years into the beginning of a reality, for it was during his administration that definite and affirmative action was inaugurated. The policy of building a canal having been adopted, our people, almost with one acclaim, were anxious for immediate action and became impatient in their demands that the dirt should begin to fly. No account was taken that this work was to be done in a torrid country over two thousand miles from the base of supplies, and an equal or greater distance from the men who must be brought into service for the performance of the work; nor that the country in which the Canal was to be built had few facilities with which to care for large numbers of men, having limited living quarters, inadequate water supply, and surroundings so unhealthful as to require the most thorough sanitation before work on a gigantic scale could be seriously considered; that the question of building a sea-level canal or a canal operating with locks had to be decided, and many other problems of equal importance had to be settled before the great work of construction could be pushed rapidly forward.

As we greet tonight the great engineer, who, with his loyal forces, has now brought this enormous enterprise to an almost completed state, we should not forget that in overcoming these preliminary troubles which were necessary in order to render the enormous work possible, great credit is due to the Isthmian Canal Commission appointed by President Roosevelt, of which Mr. Theodore P. Shonts was chairman, and to those associated with him, and with members of the Commission, like Colonel Gorgas and others, because it was under their direction that the work of sanitation and the construction of waterways, the building of houses and villages, was begun and carried forward. In fact, it was due to their efforts that the modern state was converted out of a tropical wilderness, scourged by fever and pestilence, and uninhabitable by individuals of other climates.

With all these preliminary questions settled during these first years of activity, it was then possible to proceed in a great way with the actual construction of the Canal. For the past five years the army of toilers, under the guidance of the great engineer who is our guest tonight, have been carrying on the work of construction necessary, rapidly and efficiently, until it is now practically finished. Without ostentation or display, free from political intrigue or hint of scandal, with no boastings of what he was going to do, Colonel Goethals has pursued his work, with the results accomplished that command the affectionate regard of all his countrymen and the admiration of the world.

It gives me great pleasure, members of the Economic Club, to present Colonel Goethals.

Edgar L. Schnadig presents
Gerald Wendt

A distinguished science educator and editor, Gerald Wendt was introduced at a Rotary Club luncheon in 1942 in Chicago by Edgar L. Schnadig, business educator, former president of Alden's, Inc., Chicago.

SCIENCE TODAY is serious business. It reminds me of the story of the
psychopathic patient who suffered from the hallucination that he
had a cat in his insides. Unable to disprove this, the psychiatrist
simulated an operation. When the man came out of the ether, he
was shown a black cat, and was told his troubles were over. He replied, "I'm sorry, doctor, but the cat that is bothering me is gray."

So it is with science today. You reach for a cat called U-235, and
you come up with a flock of kittens called neptunium, plutonium,
uranium 233 or something else. Like a Chicago winter, the elements
are overpowered. The alchemist of old, the first nuclear scientist,
on his deathbed begged for one more day to discover the secrets of
the universe. Now scientists produce secrets of which the universe
never dreamed.

Our speaker today is Dr. Gerald Wendt, who knows about science as it is, and as it may be. Dr. Wendt has been a professor of
chemistry at the University of Chicago, dean of the Pennsylvania
State College, director of the Battelle Institute of Industrial Research
at Columbus, Ohio. He has been a scientist in the government service, and editor and author. Dr. Wendt was born in Davenport, Iowa,
and received his professional degree at Harvard. He completed his
training in war plants, and has traveled extensively in Europe.

Dr. Wendt is author and editor of numerous textbooks in several
sciences. His best-known book is *Science for the World of Tomorrow*, published when he was director of science at the World's Fair
in New York. As consulting editor to *Time, Life, Fortune,* and *March*

of Time, his interpretation of scientific news reached a wide audience. *The Atomic Age* by Dr. Wendt appeared in 1945, ten days after the bomb hit Hiroshima. His pet phrase is "The best is yet to come," and so it is. I am proud to present, and you will be happy to hear, Dr. Gerald Wendt, editorial director of *Science Illustrated.*

Joseph M. Gwinn presents
Charles Lindbergh

Lindbergh made the first solo nonstop transatlantic flight from New York to Paris, May 20–21, 1927, in his famous plane "The Spirit of St. Louis." He was introduced at the sixty-sixth annual meeting of the National Education Association, March 1, 1928, by Joseph M. Gwinn, president of the Department of Superintendence of the NEA.

I WISH to call attention to the fact that I have a new gavel tonight. This has been presented to the president of the Department of Superintendence by Admiral Andrews. It is made of wood from the old ship "Constitution." I wish to thank Admiral Andrews and all those who are interested in the great program to rehabilitate that grand old ship. I shall prize this gavel.

If I may be permitted to take liberties with a line or two of a beautiful poem of a Scottish bard, I would say:

> Oh! Young Lochinvar is come out of the West,
> Through all the wide border his steed was the best;
> And save a smile and a stout heart he credentials had none,
> He rode all unarmed and he rode all alone.

It is a far call from swimming the Eshe River when ford there was none by the first Lochinvar to leaping the broad Atlantic where bridge there was none by our Lochinvar. It is a far call from the one fair Ellen whom Scott's Lochinvar carried away behind him to the millions that follow in the train of our Lochinvar.

He flew not alone to Paris but into the affections, ideals, and aspirations of the youth of the land, into the plans of governments and into the programs of business, industry, and trade. His achievements have so powerfully stirred the mind and emotions of youth and have so tremendously influenced the adult world of business, industry, and government that education, which must ever respond to the changes that come, must give attention to aviation. So, this program has been proposed as a beginning on aeronautical education.

The Department of Superintendence of the National Education Association is highly honored to have on this program as one of the speakers the man who made this program necessary, Colonel Charles Lindbergh.

STATESMEN

Walter Prescott Webb presents

Harry S. Truman

Former President Truman was scheduled as the principal speaker at the 1955 annual meeting of the Mississippi Valley Historical Association. At the last minute he sent word that he would be unable to attend. It is not recorded what the six hundred assembled historians said on this occasion but this imaginative and witty introduction to the speaker was fortunately preserved and published later. The introduction was prepared by the late Walter Prescott Webb, Distinguished Professor of History at the University of Texas and an authority on the American West.

IT IS A CUSTOM, almost an inviolable law, to introduce a speaker to his audience. The assumption is that the audience has little knowledge of the speaker and needs to be told who he is, what he has done, and what may be expected of him. I cannot act on this assumption tonight. I prefer a truer one, namely, that this audience knows a great deal more about the speaker than he knows about the audience. Therefore, Mr. Truman, I am reversing the customary procedure by introducing the audience to the speaker.

Your audience tonight comprises the members of that profession whose business it is to teach American history to the American people, mainly the youth, and to the world. This is the national organization of American historians. They, and their successors, examine critically all the evidence left by the men who make history and also the evidence left by the contemporaries of the principals. In the long run it is difficult to hide very much from prying eyes for they have the patience to await the emergence of the documents and the whole truth. In a sense they tend the scales of justice, and see that the makers of history are given honest weight.

It is not often that one of the principals of history appears before this body. Your appearance here tonight is therefore of more than

193

usual importance. You will be listened to with attention, and what you say will be retailed in a thousand classrooms to tens of thousands of university and college students within a week. It is my guess that in this re-presentation you will be dealt with more objectively than you have sometimes been in the past.

The members of this audience are especially interested in the reports that you are now using your supposed leisure for compiling and writing an account of your own experience in national and world affairs during one of the most tempestuous periods of the past two centuries. We trust that the reports are true, and that nothing interferes with this plan. It is unfortunate that so few of the leading makers of history have had the inclination to record their observations on their own stirring times.

When I heard that you had turned historian, I thought what a fine thing it would be to bring Mr. Truman to the university to teach young people about American political life. How the students would flock to your classes. But when I took a second look at the local situation, I decided that the plan was not at this time very practical. I think I should prepare you for what may happen to you after your performance tonight. Teachers are getting scarce, and many of the members of this audience are here to recruit men of promise. If you do well tonight, you are likely to be offered a job if you will make yourself available. The pay won't be very good, but I'll tell you one thing. You will have the best tenure you have had since you got out of the army.

Finally, Mr. Truman, I want to take advantage of this opportunity to express a personal grievance. In 1948 you caused me to lose a whole night's sleep. My grievance was heightened next day when I read in the papers that you went to bed at ten o'clock. It seems to me that in a crisis like that you should be more sympathetic. The next night I slept fine, but some of the best people in Texas, according to Dun & Bradstreet rating, did not go to sleep for two weeks.

I think I speak for this entire Association, meeting here in your state in the heart of this great nation, when I say that your presence here makes this a memorable occasion.

Ladies and Gentlemen: Mr. Truman.

Joseph W. Martin presents
Sam Rayburn

Sam Rayburn (1882–1961) entered the United States House of Representatives in 1913 and served there until his death. He was introduced at the First Session of the 82d Congress, January 3, 1951, by Joseph W. Martin, Jr. (1884–1968), long-time permanent chairman of the Republican National Convention, member of Congress 1925–1966, and Speaker of the House in 1947–1948 and 1953–1954.

MY COLLEAGUES, it is a privilege for me to stand on this exalted platform, even if it is only for a few moments. It is one of the compensations of a defeated candidate; he is permitted to share in the reflected glory of the victor. I admit that several months ago I had ideas I might occupy this position a little longer than I am going to today; the decision has been otherwise, however, and I have no regrets. But, seriously, it is a happy place assigned to me.

Ten years ago the Members of this House elected a Speaker. He has served with one interruption, which I might say with the indulgence of the Speaker, was a happy interlude. He has now been chosen for a sixth term. On January 30 of this year he will have served as Speaker of the House longer than any other man in American history. The record previously was held by that able, distinguished, and most notable son of Kentucky, Henry Clay. On January 30 our Speaker will have exceeded his tenure of office.

One cannot be elected Speaker for all that period of time without being a fine character, a man of extraordinary ability, great fairness, and a parliamentarian par excellence. Those are virtues which we have in our Speaker. In this hour of confusion, this hour of uncertainty when none of us knows what the future has ahead, we have a man who has the courage; we have a man who has the firmness to do that which is right, to the end that our country may emerge a better country. We are sometimes misunderstood by our friends in other countries. We fight, we debate, we vote, and then we settle the question. They cannot understand that these are the practical principles that make for a democracy, a republic. They cannot see either that when our fight is over, that when we reach a decision, we are all united, we are all Americans with but one thought: to make America a better land for all our people.

So, Ladies and Gentlemen, without further ado, it gives me great pleasure to present to you your Speaker and my Speaker, the Honorable Sam Rayburn, of Texas.

Adlai E. Stevenson presents
Lyndon B. Johnson

Beyond reasonable doubt, Adlai E. Stevenson (1900–1965) was America's most gifted speaker of the past two decades. Shortly after the 1962 Cuban missile crisis, he introduced President Kennedy at a banquet as the author, producer, and star of Mr. Khrushchev's new play, "A Funny Thing Happened to Me on My Way to Cuba." In 1964 he introduced President Johnson at a Washington banquet.

MR. PRESIDENT, you are doing so well that even the Republicans like you. They can find only two things wrong — your foreign policy and your domestic policy.

Samuel L. Clemens presents
Winston Churchill

When Winston Churchill, fresh from his war experience among the Boers, spoke at the Waldorf in New York, December 12, 1900, he was introduced by Samuel L. Clemens. There was a good deal of pro-Boer sentiment in New York and his introduction was no endorsement. He began by saying that Churchill knew a great deal about war but nothing about peace. He then went on to say:

ALTHOUGH I think England sinned in getting into a war in South Africa which she could have avoided without loss of credit or dignity — just as I think we have sinned in crowding ourselves into a war in the Philippines on the same terms.

Mr. Churchill will tell you about the war in South Africa, and he is competent — he fought and wrote through it himself. And he made a record there which would be a proud one for a man twice his age. By his father he is English, by his mother he is American — to my mind the blend which makes the perfect man. We are now on the friendliest and pleasantest terms with England. Mainly through my missionary efforts I suppose; and I am glad. We have always been kin: kin in blood, kin in religion, kin in representative government, kin in ideals, kin in just and lofty purposes; and now we are kin in sin, the harmony is complete, like Mr. Churchill himself. I have the honor to present him to you.

Alfred Hayes presents
Indira Gandhi

In the spring of 1966, Her Excellency Indira Gandhi made her first visit to the United States as Prime Minister of India. In New York she delivered a policy speech before the members and guests of the Economic Club of New York. Alfred Hayes, president of the Federal Reserve Bank of New York and president of the Club, presented her to the audience.

OUR SPEAKER tonight is the head of government of the world's second most populous nation. She speaks for an ancient country to which we in the West look for much of our heritage of civilization. But more importantly, she speaks for a country which we believe is one of the great hopes of tomorrow's world. Those of us who have visited India have been impressed both by the vastness of its problems and by the importance to the world of their successful solution.

It is no small task to follow in the footsteps of those two brilliant and revered leaders who were in large measure responsible for the emergence of India in this century as a major independent nation. I am speaking, of course, of Mahatma Gandhi and Jawaharlal Nehru, the father of our honored guest. After them, how would India find the leadership needed to sustain it on the path of democracy? Even those who know little about India have the instinctive feeling that the right choice has been made.

It would be presumptuous on my part to try to summarize Mrs. Gandhi's distinguished career, and I know you are impatient to get to the main event of tonight's program. Most of you have read about Mrs. Gandhi's steady rise to political eminence. Certainly she received the best kind of training for her vast responsibilities: as a militant young activist and disciple of Mahatma Gandhi in the noncooperation movement; as a student at Oxford privileged to see the best of Western culture and to view India in perspective; as a member and later as a high official of the Indian National Congress; as a participant in all kinds of social work; as Minister of Information and Broadcasting; and as official hostess and unofficial confidante of her illustrious father. In these and other capacities, she achieved a broad understanding of India's goals and India's problems.

While it would be foolish to overlook her debt to a great father — in natural traits, in an awareness of the importance of service and sacrifice, and in exposure to his wise judgments — the striking fact is that Mrs. Gandhi achieved much of her success through her own merit.

If I have not stressed the fact that India's Prime Minister is a woman, it is because she has won recognition as a statesman in full competition with many able men, and not primarily as a representative of her sex. Nevertheless I am sure she will forgive this virtually all-male audience if we find some special inspiration in the fact that besides all of her other accomplishments, she is a very charming woman as well. It is to India's everlasting credit that Mrs. Gandhi has not been hampered by the prejudices that still handicap her sex is so many parts of the world. Interestingly enough, equal opportunity for women has certainly not been characteristic of India over the centuries; and it has been only through the efforts of leaders such as Mr. Nehru and Mrs. Gandhi herself that India has advanced to the front rank of nations in this respect.

Ladies and Gentlemen, it is with the greatest pleasure that I present to you a person of talent, charm and dignity, a many-faceted human being, Her Excellency Indira Gandhi, Prime Minister of India.

Arthur K. Watson presents
William W. Scranton

Arthur K. Watson, chairman of the IBM World Trade Corporation, presented Governor William W. Scranton of Pennsylvania to members and guests of the Economic Club of New York on March 3, 1964. To appreciate the flavor of the introduction, one should keep in mind that 1964 was a presidential year and that Governor Scranton was being mentioned as a possible draft choice of the Republican Convention. One should also recall that Mr. Watson and Governor Scranton had been friends from their student days at Hotchkiss and Yale.

To GET anything out of our next speaker, they say, you've got to talk economic development with him — and, preferably, economic development in Pennsylvania.

But don't make the mistake of thinking you can turn the talk around. Pennsylvania he'll talk about. Pennsylvania Avenue he won't. I know because I tried.

Governor Scranton may be the only Yale man to have won his "Y" through reluctance. When he was urged to run for Congress, he was a reluctant candidate. Later when he was urged to run for governor of Pennsylvania, he again was a reluctant candidate. The opposition is still wondering how much worse it would have been had he been ambitious.

More than most men, Governor Scranton is aware of what Theodore H. White has called *the* political problem of twentieth century technology: how to make it possible for communities of human beings to withstand the shocks of industrial change.

His earlier years were spent in helping to rescue the now vigorous city that bears his family name. From Harrisburg, he is presently directing a statewide effort to the same end: to restore to the Commonwealth of Pennsylvania its tradition of greatness and build it a place in the future.

Our speaker has described himself as a fiscal conservative, a liberal on civil rights, an internationalist in foreign matters, and a pragmatist on most everything else. He has a reputation for applying common sense to the solution of difficult problems. He has the good balance of an expert skier, which he is.

Before presenting the Governor, I'm going to ask the Waldorf to turn up the heat just a bit. I wouldn't want anyone to feel there's a draft in the room.

The Governor's subject will be: "The Republican Challenge — A Call to Leadership."

Gentlemen, the distinguished Governor of Pennsylvania.

Jerome P. Cavanagh presents
George Alfred Brown

The Right Honourable George Alfred Brown, Secretary of State for Foreign Affairs of the United Kingdom since 1966, spoke to the Economic Club of Detroit on October 13, 1966. He was introduced by the Mayor of the City of Detroit.

I AM MOST delighted that I was asked to introduce our guest of honor today. I think at this most crucial time in our history — and when I say "our" I don't just mean America's, I mean the world's — we are very deeply honored in this city by the presence of the Right Honourable George Brown, Foreign Secretary and Deputy Prime Minister of Great Britain. He has come to us, as I am sure most of you know, directly from some meetings with some of the leaders of the world in New York. He made a magnificent address — which I am sure some of you had the opportunity to listen to — earlier this week before the General Assembly of the United Nations, in which he called for the Soviet Union to join with Great Britain in reconvening the Geneva Conference.

He met twice, as most of us know, with Foreign Minister Gromyko in New York to discuss Vietnam and prospects for a treaty, too, to ban the spread of nuclear weapons. Also, he is scheduled to talk later this week with our President and with the Secretary of State. These very delicate and at the same time most important discussions will, I am sure all of us hope and trust, lead to what we all seek — a peaceful world.

I might add that Mr. Brown's voice is a very refreshing one in diplomatic circles, where, sometimes, great emphasis is placed upon saying nothing at all in a very convincing manner. Earlier this week I was most amused during a press conference, I believe it was on the Huntley-Brinkley show, in which their guest of honor replied to a

203

question that was posed by a newsman, saying with characteristic diplomacy: "I can't answer that: it's damned silly."

Mr. Brown comes from a British arena of politics in which you must be as good at handling a street heckler as you are in your handling of grave international problems. I think you will find his observations today both fair and frank. This same frankness led to a rather celebrated row during the mid-fifties that I am sure many of us remember, when Khrushchev and Bulganin first visited England.

Those two Russian leaders set aside some time to meet with the Labour party leadership. Mr. Brown was among the leadership that was meeting with these two Russian leaders and, as an old trade union leader, he bawled out Mr. Khrushchev about the Russian treatment of unions, and it became rather celebrated in England. The Russians, needless to say — at least in that point in time — were not used to such words.

It is true that Britain today is having some difficulties, but I think there is bound to be a certain amount of trouble running any country, as Mr. Brown can attest. As has been said in the past, if you're a president or a prime minister, the trouble happens to you; but if you're a tyrant you can arrange things so that most of the trouble happens to other people.

We're extremely grateful today to Mr. Brown for consenting to be here with us and we pray for the success of his mission in this country. May I at this time introduce to all of you the Right Honourable George Brown.

Harry S. Ashmore presents
J. William Fulbright

At a convocation staged by the Center for the Study of Democratic Institutions on May 10, 1966, Senator Fulbright was introduced by Harry S. Ashmore, journalist, adviser to Adlai E. Stevenson during his presidential campaigns, and a director of the Fund for the Republic, Inc.

THE CENTER for the Study of Democratic Institutions claims to be an educational institution. Our fiscal kinship with the private university is evident; we too are mendicants, subsisting as the tax-free beneficiary of a variety of supporters who share our faith in the public dialogue.

The Center is often described as a university without students. It is true that there is a faculty of sorts up at Santa Barbara, and some of its concerns are academic. But if there are no students on Eucalyptus Hill it does not follow that the small resident company is engaged in a happy process of self-education. The Center's address is outward, to an audience of peers, and its aspiration is to widen the circles of discussion of the basic issues of our time.

This description applies almost as well to our speaker today. He too could be classified as a somewhat unconventional educational institution — a man who wears the mantle of lawmaker but perhaps serves us best in the role of tutor and critic.

We see him today, as we have seen him before, standing almost alone against the insensate drift of public policy that has pushed us beyond into the holocaust. So he stood at the time of the Bay of Pigs, and in that garish season when the late Joe McCarthy brought the entire process of government to a brutal point of disorder.

These lonely heights are characteristic of the whole of Senator Fulbright's remarkable public career. They loom above the quiet, productive stretches of his twenty-six years in Washington — the times of persistent plugging in the areas of his special concern: international organization, the free flow of ideas, and education, all of these coming together in the notable foreign exchange program that bears his name. The motive power is a kind of stubborn morality that time and again has sent him into the lists against political giants. That familiar portrait of the professorial inquisitor, with his glasses on the end of his nose, was first imprinted on the national consciousness way back in the Truman administration, when he turned a sharp eye on the Reconstruction Finance Corporation.

It is the reflexes of the educator that call Senator Fulbright to his often onerous duty. He began as a professor of law and served briefly as President of the University of Arkansas. But, as I suspect, he always knew what he has long since proved — that education and politics are inseparable. When the Center staged the first of these major convocations in New York in 1963 to consider "The Challenges to Democracy," it was inevitable that the Senator would be called upon as a principal participant. Indeed, I would say that in any gathering called to consider serious matters of general concern to the republic his presence would be welcome, and might be indispensable. Certainly this is true of a meeting devoted to critical consideration of the University in America.

As an old constituent, I am particularly pleased to give you the junior Senator from Arkansas, J. William Fulbright.

Hugh Bullock presents
Lester B. Pearson

A dinner to honor the Right Honourable Lester B. Pearson, then Prime Minister of Canada, was given by the Pilgrims of the United States, November 6, 1963, New York. Hugh Bullock, president of the Pilgrims, presided and made the introduction.

As HISTORIANS look back some day and endeavor to arrange the year 1963 in its proper perspective, there is no doubt that they will record as one of the major events of the world we live in the unforeseen, inconsiderate, unconscionable rout of a baseball team called the New York Yankees by Westerners — from Brooklyn!

Even the Prime Minister of Canada was affected by this (I have no idea how much financially). But he must have followed this important event with more than normal interest because he is a ball player himself, and a very good one. In fact he is the only Prime Minister Canada ever had or that any other country ever had who was formerly paid money for playing baseball on a semipro basis.

But being a Canadian why shouldn't he be a hockey player? That he is, too, and good enough to have beaten Cambridge as an Oxford Blue and to have played on the British Olympic Hockey Team. He used to be a crack athlete, and even after his undergraduate days, coached varsity hockey and football at the University of Toronto.

He met his wife at the University of Toronto under circumstances that greatly displeased his fellow lecturers in history. They noticed that Mr. Pearson had somehow appropriated the job of assigning senior history students to the various seminars. They were indignant that the prettiest girls always ended up in his own seminar. Then within two years, he married the prettiest of them all. She still is — Mrs. Pearson!

What were the beginnings of this man whom his tutor at Oxford called "an extraordinary young man, a tremendous idealist?"

Well, he was born on St. George's Day near the end of the last century near Toronto — the son of a Methodist minister. And his touchstones have always been the Christian principles which have been taught in our churches. After his schooling at the University of Toronto and Oxford and his teaching career, he joined the Department of External Affairs and for the next thirty-five years served his country.

He had already served his country — and gallantly — during World War I. Indeed, his nickname came from this war where he enlisted, was posted to Egypt, the Balkans, and served on the Salonika front for a year and a half. He earned his commission, then transferred to the Royal Flying Corps. Here a senior officer didn't think his official name was belligerent enough and saw fit to substitute another.

In 1939 he was convinced World War II was coming and insisted on being in London when it was declared and during Dunkirk and the blitz. After a stretch in Ottawa he was Minister and then tremendously effective Canadian Ambassador in Washington.

After the war he was made Under Secretary of State but in 1948 was persuaded by Prime Minister St. Laurent to enter politics and take over the portfolio of Secretary of State for External Affairs. Here he added to the luster of his country's name in the chancelleries of the world.

He headed the Canadian delegation to nine sessions of the General Assembly of the United Nations. He was president of the seventh session of the General Assembly. Twice he was the choice of important nations to be the Secretary General of the United Nations.

He drafted the historic speech that first suggested NATO. He guided through the Assembly the plan that created the state of Israel. During the Suez crisis he suggested the United Nations force.

In 1957 he won the Nobel Peace Prize — and the world thought it highly deserved. It is only one of many honors. He holds an enviable British decoration. The last I heard he held twenty-six honorary degrees. There are probably more by now.

But with it all he is an extraordinarily able and prominent man with no false pride; with dignity, but not arthritic dignity, and with a delightful sense of humor.

He has a magic knack for getting on with people. He is an intellectual, a stern idealist, yes, but above all he is a warm and charming human being. His friends — not acquaintances, friends — are legion.

This is the best known Canadian in the world. This is the best liked Canadian in the world. The Chief of State of our gallant ally, a nation and a people for whom we have the deepest admiration.

Ladies and Gentlemen, the Prime Minister of Canada, the Right Honourable Lester B. Pearson!

Everett McKinley Dirksen presents

Robert A. Taft

Senator Everett McKinley Dirksen nominated Senator Robert A. Taft (1889–1953) for President at the twenty-fifth Republican convention in 1952 at Chicago.

MR. CHAIRMAN, Fellow Delegates and Fellow Americans: I hope you will be quiet for just a minute to hear my case.

. . . .

The first test of a winner is whether he has steadily, consistently won. From the time he first sought public office in 1921, the man I shall give you has been winning without exception. Thirty-one years of continuous victory is an unparalleled recommendation for a winner.

But there is another and more formidable test, and that is to consider the source of the votes from which victory must come. The name I shall present to you will have great appeal for a vast group.

. . . .

He can take it. His life has been like a show case into which all may peer, and from now until November nothing can be said to asperse him that has not already been uttered. Does he have character? He is not only Mr. Republican. He is also Mr. Integrity, this virtue alone can light us down the road of a faded faith and restore confidence to our people before it is too late.

. . . .

And so, my friends and fellow delegates, I present one whom many esteem as the amiable ambassador of our last best hope. I present one who is valiant for truth. I present a defender of the Republican faith. I present Mr. Republican, Mr. Integrity, Mr. American. I present Bob Taft.

Harry S. Truman presents
Winston Churchill

On March 5, 1946, the Honourable Winston Churchill, Prime Minister of Great Britain, made his famous speech "The Sinews of Peace" at Westminster College, Fulton, Missouri. He was introduced on this occasion by Harry S. Truman, then President of the United States. Phil M. Donnelly, former Governor of Missouri and Frank L. McCluer, former President of Westminster College, are referred to in the introduction.

You KNOW, this is one of the greatest pleasures and privileges I have had since I have been President of the United States. I appreciate most highly Governor Donnelly's welcome to Mr. Churchill and myself, and I am very thankful that Dr. McCluer suggested to me that Mr. Churchill be invited to deliver this lecture today.

I had a letter from Mr. Churchill — oh, six months ago or more — in which he said he was considering a vacation in the United States or in North Africa. I sent him Dr. McCluer's invitation and made a long-hand note on the bottom of it telling him that if he would spend his vacation in the United States, at whatever point he chose to pick, and then would deliver this lecture, I would make it a point to come to Missouri and personally welcome him and introduce him for that lecture.

I had never met Mr. Churchill personally until the Berlin Conference between Mr. Stalin, Mr. Churchill, and myself. I became very fond of both of them. They are men, and they are leaders in this world today when we need leadership. It is a pleasure to me to introduce Mr. Churchill. He is one of the great men of the age. He is a great Englishman, but he is half American.

Mr. Churchill and I believe in freedom of speech. I understand that Mr. Churchill is going to talk on "The Sinews of Peace." I know that he will have something constructive to say to the world in that speech. I am happy that he came here to deliver it, and it is one of the great privileges of my lifetime to be able to present to you that great world citizen, Mr. Churchill.

Will Rogers presents
Franklin Delano Roosevelt

On the evening of September 24, 1932, at Olympic Stadium, Los Angeles, Governor Roosevelt of New York, the 1932 Democratic presidential nominee, attended a "motion picture and sport pageant" to raise funds for the Marion Davies Foundation for Crippled Children. The actor and humorist Will Rogers (1879–1935) introduced him and in his opening remarks referred to the refusal of the Republican mayor of Los Angeles to welcome Roosevelt because he "is a wet and I am a dry." Rogers refers to the Hollywood Bowl, where Roosevelt had made a campaign speech during the afternoon.

I KNOW you all expect me to introduce our distinguished guest because I'm the only mayor around here who is on speaking terms with him.

This, Governor, is a wonderful crowd. We must have eighty thousand or ninety thousand people here, the most people who ever paid to see a politician. I'd even introduce Hoover if he'd come here.

Hollywood Bowl is located between Hollywood and Beverly, the Sodom and Gomorrah of the Orange Juice Belt. The bowl is dedicated to amusement and rattlesnakes. But the charter is very liberal and doesn't say that a politician cant enter and politic. They will rent it to a nudist convention if they will pay the rent.

Now Franklyn (by the way, are you by any means related to Benjamin Franklyn, the man that I think invented the steamboat?) . . . Then you have taken the name of Delano. That of course was to catch the Italian vote. You cant by any means ring in Goldberg, can you? Well, Franklyn, I can call you that for I have known you for many years, long before your governorship, or even your Secretary of Navyship. In fact, I have known you since babyhood. I knew you since you first started nominating Al Smith for something or other.

213

You have spent a lifetime nominating Al Smith. You used to come to the *Follies* as a young man — in fact as an old man too — and I would call on you from the stage to say a few words, perhaps in appreciation of Mr. Ziegfeld's show, and you would arise and for no reason at all nominate Al Smith for something. But I know Al in the goodness and generosity of his heart appreciates all that and will never forget it and will repay you for it.

Let us hope he does it before election.

But to get away from all this piffle talk and back to fundamentals and the Democratic party. I wont say a word here tonight about your "forgotten man." For every man in America thinks you were referring to him.

We have always been tremendously fortunate in picking candidates in both political parties for President what are men of high character. And this time is no exception.

Our national political conventions, if you have ever attended one or heard it over the radio, are nothing but glorified Mickey Mouse cartoons, and are solely for amusement purposes. But by the grace of some divine providence they do always give forth two excellent candidates.

Governor Roosevelt — you are here tonight the guest of people who spend their lives trying to entertain. This great gathering is neither creed or politics, Jew or Gentile, Democrat or Republican, whether they vote for you or not and thousands of them wont (never mind what they tell you). Every one of them admire you as a man. Your platform, your policies, your plans may not meet with their approval, but your high type of manhood gains the admiration of every person in this audience.

So we meet not Roosevelt the candidate, but a neighbor from the other side of the Rocky Mountains. This introduction may have lacked logic, and particularly floweriness, but you must remember, you are only a candidate. Come back when you are President and I will do better. I am wasting no oratory on a mere prospect.

Richard Olney presents Woodrow Wilson

Woodrow Wilson (1856–1924) was graduated from Princeton in 1879 and became president of his alma mater in 1902. He entered public life as Governor of New Jersey in 1911. On the occasion of his address before the City Club of Boston, January 27, 1912, he was introduced by Richard Olney, Secretary of State during the administration of President Grover Cleveland. Wilson was elected President of the United States the following November.

I RECOGNIZE the part I am to play on this occasion and will at once relieve you of any apprehension that I am going to occupy any considerable portion of your time.

This club is nonpartisan, which means, I take it, not that a party man is barred out, but only that neither is his opponent or critic barred out. New Jersey has lent us her governor who in less than two years' time has become a national figure of the first magnitude and whose name is now a household word from one end of the country to the other. If I may indicate very generally and briefly the characteristics of so short and yet so distinguished a career, I begin by asking you to note one which every citizen wants to see in every public man, be he of his own party or any other, and that is the capacity for leadership. The speech or the writing or the act even is as nothing to the man behind it and to the impression he makes of sincerity, trustworthiness, and general sanity of mind and thought. Be the merits of the great fight in the New Jersey Legislature of 1911 what they may, it brought out a sturdy and sagacious leadership, which won the admiration and respect of foes and the permanent confidence of friends.

There may be, of course, a wrong leadership as well as a right, and when the leadership of a great political party in a free country is concerned, what will be the evidence that the leadership will be wise, that it will rise to the height of great social and political problems; that on the one hand it will not be led away by the abstractions of the doctrinaire, nor on the other hand fail to recognize and apply the essential principles of all popular government? On that point no other or greater assurance is possible than that the leadership shall be a thoroughly educated and informed leadership, a result possible only if the leader shall have made the principles of political science the subject of the closest thought and study and shall have familiarized himself with the history of their application in his own country.

Finally, we live in times when not the foundation but the superstructure of our political house seems to be shaken by the winds of strange doctrines. The foundation is democratic and is solid and means government by the people for the people. But there is intense and wide-spread dissatisfaction because the claim and belief that our vaunted government by the people for the people is, in fact, government by a class for a class. The present and burning question for statesmanship is, What is the remedy? Is it less democracy or more democracy? Just what shape the prescription shall take — just what measures shall restore to the people their proper power over their own government — is a question over which men may honestly differ, will certainly exhaust the resources of the highest statesmanship, and, perhaps, will never be truly and finally answered until after a period of long and painful experiment.

I am about to present to you a man whose life work thus far is a conspicuous exhibit of the traits and convictions and accomplishments to which I have briefly referred. I am presenting him, not as a high official, nor as a candidate, nor as a Democrat, but as an American citizen entitled to the respect and esteem of men of whatever political faith; as a man who has made good wherever he has been tried; who has proved his possession of the inestimable gift of leadership; who has vindicated the claims to regard of the "scholar in politics"; who, sensible of the abuses which have come to disfigure the administration of popular government, has lost not a jot of faith in popular government itself; and who is of the type of men in whom lies the best hope for the country's future. I may add that he has a capacity and propensity for telling the truth, which is not always to the advantage or satisfaction of those who ask for it.

James Hamilton Lewis presents
Jacob M. Dickinson

Jacob M. Dickinson (1851–1928) served as Secretary of War in the cabinet of President Taft and was a lawyer by profession. He was introduced at the twenty-fourth annual banquet of the Iroquois Club of Chicago May 10, 1905, by James Hamilton Lewis, United States Senator from Illinois.

WE READ in the *Christian Advocate* that a little boy in Tennessee, answering his examination in anatomy, defined the spinal column as "a long wriggly bone running down a man's back, with the man's head and brains settin' on one end, and the man hisse'f settin' on the other." Tennessee claims to be the backbone of the South. We grant her that function. And while she sits upon that end of consolation, we remind her that the head and brains of the other end have been transferred to the shoulders of Chicago. And while we accept the hostage with the acclaim of a proud conqueror, nevertheless we hear the moan of his first mother as she wails out, in the words of his favorite *Odyssey*, "Ulysses is gone, and there's none left in Ithaca to bend his bow." I have the honor to present to the toast that national statesman, international lawyer and orator, former distinguished Tennesseean, now illustrious Illinoisan, Honorable J. M. Dickinson.

Leon Fraser presents

James F. Byrnes

James F. Byrnes, former governor of South Carolina, was Justice of the United States Supreme Court (1941–1942), director of the Office of War Mobilization during World War II, and later Secretary of State (July 1945–January 1947). On the occasion of his speech before the Academy of Political Science, April 12, 1944, he was introduced by Leon Fraser, president of the First National Bank of New York.

It is a little hard to know just how to introduce the next speaker. I was wondering what could be said, and then it occurred to me that perhaps one of the things that we are fighting for in this war is that free men may have the kind of self-made career the next speaker has had. Brought up (he will pardon my saying so, I hope) without the handicap of higher education, and without an undue amount of lower education, he became by working hard in a law office an able and an eminent lawyer in his state, so able and so affable, in fact, that the voters decided that they would send him to the lower house of the Congress of the United States. There they liked him so much that they decided that he had better go to the upper house. After he had been in the upper house for a while, somebody said, "Well, does anybody think about the Supreme Court of the United States for this gentleman?" Somebody did. Then he became Justice of the Supreme Court.

He has not been out of Washington to make an address for two years, except once; and the fact that he comes here tonight is, I think, a compliment from him which we in New York City duly appreciate. Many of us in New York go frequently to Washington, but those in Washington who have had some indirect connection with the New Deal do not come so often out of Washington. I am not suggesting, of course, that Mr. Justice Byrnes hesitated to come out because he had had some connection with the New Deal.

I could introduce him as Mr. Justice Byrnes, Mr. Senator Byrnes, Director of the Office of War Mobilization, former Congressman, former lawyer, eminent Southerner, and yet perhaps it would be simpler to introduce him by the name by which he is best known to all his friends (and all in the telephone book are his friends, every one of them), and they know him as Jimmie Byrnes.

Ladies and Gentlemen of the Academy: It is my privilege to present to you "Jimmie" Byrnes, Director of the Office of War Mobilization, who will speak upon the subject "Preparation for Peace on the Home Front."

John W. Davis presents

Lester B. Pearson

A dinner to honor Sir Campbell Stuart, chairman of the Executive Committee of the Pilgrims of Great Britain, was given by the Pilgrims of the United States, October 12, 1950, at the Hotel Plaza, New York City. John W. Davis, lawyer, former American ambassador at large to Great Britain, and president of the Pilgrims of the United States, presided and introduced the Honourable Lester B. Pearson, who was then a member of the Canadian Parliament and president of the seventh session of the United Nations General Assembly.

THE FIRST speaker whom I will have the privilege of presenting to you is doubly welcome. He is welcome not only because of his personal achievements and his familiarity with this country; he is welcome, also, as a representative of a great and friendly neighbor. He has behind him a variegated and a brilliant life; in the Canadian Army during World War I; professor of history some time after that event; Minister Counselor, Canadian Embassy in Washington; Minister Plenipotentiary in Washington; the Ambassador of Canada to the United States. He has, therefore, not only taught history, but he has made it, and has been the collaborator in a series of international conferences that I would tremble to enumerate. Everywhere his service has been marked by the utmost brilliance, accompanied by the greatest sanity.

He comes to us from our great neighbor in the north who sits there in the vast domain from ocean to ocean, and from Maine to the mythical boundary of forty-nine degrees looks out across the Atlantic to the motherland, and then over a boundary which affords no obstacle to sight or to communication — she looks with us down over the reaches of the Mississippi to the Gulf, and beyond.

I am not going to make a speech on the undivided boundary, Mr.

Ambassador. It is a very fascinating thing that here these two people should live, comrades in war and companions in peace, divided only by a mythical line stretching from the Pacific to the Lakes and down the Lakes to the St. Lawrence, and down the St. Lawrence to the sea.

Many heroics have been spoken about that unguarded boundary. It not only has great potency as a symbol and a lesson, but like most historic events, it even has its comic occurrences. The one that seems to me to be the most comical is the year the United States spent over a million dollars restoring the fortification at Rouses Point. After that expenditure, surveyors came along and informed us that, to the great reddening of our faces, we had spent all that money on the Canadian side of the line. It was a very discouraging incident.

I present to you, Gentlemen, a man distinguished for himself, sympathetic with America and American ideals, and a representative of our great neighbor to the north, His Excellency the Honourable Lester B. Pearson, Officer of the Order of the British Empire, Member of Parliament, the Canadian Secretary of State for External Affairs.

Lewis W. Douglas presents Lord Halifax

Lord Halifax (Edward Frederick Lindley Wood) served as British Ambassador to the United States from 1941 to 1946. At the meeting of the Academy of Political Science, November 10, 1948, he was introduced as the principal speaker by Lewis W. Douglas, former American Ambassador to Great Britain, and the presiding officer on this occasion.

EACH ONE of us, I presume, establishes for himself, in anything he may undertake, a certain standard of performance by which he tries to measure his own action. About a hundred years ago in Ireland during a political campaign, a speaker, a prominent and principal speaker of an evening meeting, was introduced by the chairman of the occasion. The chairman took considerable time — according to his own standards, not too much; according to the standards of others, far too much — to introduce the distinguished orator.

When at last he took the platform to deliver his address, he reminded his audience of that old Irish legend that ran something like this: Whenever a baby is born in Ireland, it is always kissed by the fairies. If it is kissed on its eyes, it is clear evidence that when the baby reaches maturity, it will be a great artist. If it should be kissed on its ears, it is known that it will be a great musician. If on its mouth, it will be a great public speaker. "Now," said the orator of the evening, "I cannot say precisely what part of the anatomy of the chairman was kissed by the fairies, but I can say that he's a darned good chairman!"

I have been very apprehensive about performing this task this evening because I felt quite confident that I would be unable to meet that high standard of performance.

There are two phases of our task. The first is to defeat the enemy. General Hunter has dealt with one of the most important and one of the most significant of the implements of war at our hand, with which we undertake to achieve that result with a certainty that cannot be controverted. The second phase of our problem is to preserve the fruits of victory to establish an enduring peace upon enduring foundations.

It was Lord Acton, I think, who said that if knowledge of the past was considered by some to be a hindrance and an interference, it must also be recognized as the source of our emancipation. The past discloses in an undebatable fashion that political arrangements alone are not enough to preserve a peace. They are not enough to prevent resort to arms as the final court of appeals. The past discloses that these political arrangements must be integrated with other things that move human beings to action; that economic force must be molded into, welded into the structure of political arrangements.

The past suggests that no matter how perfect the political accommodations may be, commercial intercourse between nations must become unfettered, and that the handmaiden of this intercourse, an international currency of durability, must be established. And the past further suggests that we must avoid identifying the proprietary interests with the sovereignty of the state, lest what previously existed as a conflict between individuals, not having the power to resort to force, assume the character of a struggle between nation states.

These are some of the things that the past discloses and that, if recognized by us, may lead to our emancipation. But, fortunately, there is, as our distinguished guest tonight, one far better tutored in these things than I, one skilled by tradition and by training and by inheritance, the best of the best that England can produce, one of a long line of public servants dedicating their lives, as they have in the past and as he is in the present, to the welfare of his people and of the world.

Intimately associated with education, Fellow of All Souls College at Oxford, once Chancellor of that great University, he has occupied so many offices of high distinction in his own government that I would be violating the standard which I originally established if I were to undertake to recite them. Viceroy of India, Lord President of the Council, Secretary of State for War, Secretary of State for Foreign Affairs, and now British Ambassador to the Government of the United States, His Excellency Viscount Halifax!

Frederick Landis presents

Will H. Hays

Will H. Hays (1879–1934), president of Motion Picture Producers and Distributors of America, Inc. (1922–1945), took a prominent part in Republican politics in the twenties and was Postmaster General during the Harding regime. His friend and political colleague, Frederick Landis, United States congressman and newspaper columnist, introduced Mr. Hays at a meeting of the Indiana Society of Chicago, January 1921.

Mr. President and Gentlemen: The earth is still the Lord's, but not the "fullness" thereof. And so it is harder to speak to you tonight. In fact my most successful banquet speeches have been delivered to audiences that were totally unconscious.

But the law of compensation is with us. Along with Prohibition has come a larger faith in man. In the old days whenever a man reached for his hip pocket there was consternation; everybody tried to get away from him. How different it is here tonight!

Meeting for our historic purpose, we naturally think of the historic anniversary just past. A little over three hundred years ago the Pilgrims came to establish a land where every man could worship his Maker according to the dictates of his wife's conscience. How the American Soul has flourished in the balmy climate of liberty! One room was enough for the religious needs of the Pilgrims, but it takes five thousand golf courses to accommodate the Sunday devotions of their pious descendants. A little while ago spirituality seemed lost in a multitude of frivolities; men seemed to have forgotten their Creator, but now we hear them calling to him from behind every bunker from Maine to California!

This Society had trouble in securing a guest of honor for tonight. First of all they came to see me about it, but as a Progressive who had just finished making speeches for Harding, I felt that was as much as any one man should be asked to submit to. So I suggested Bill Hays. The Committee said: "What if this Senatorial Investigating Committee 'lands' on him? We don't want any guest of honor who may throw us down by being arrested right in the middle of the soup course!"

But I said: "Don't worry; they may get some of them, but they'll never get Bill!" I had faith in him — faith in his integrity and faith in his marvelous interference.

I knew that he had been successful in politics for twenty years and never had been caught at it.

And I knew that he had too fine a conception of the moral obligation of a church elder to let anybody catch him with the goods on him!

But the Committee said: "Just to play safe, let's put the dinner off till January."

Then came the election and the Investigating Committee adjourned *sine die!* But Bill was ready for it. He actually came through with a deficit! Nobody knows how he managed to do it, but he had the books to prove it.

It was as if he had spent two years in a livery stable and come forth with an aroma of heliotrope!

Other leaders have given us victory, but Bill Hays is the first one who ever gave us respectability. After "saving the country" we always used to bathe in concentrated lye, but this time we went forth, calling Democrats to repentance!

It is a wonderful thing for millions of Republicans to be reborn after a lifetime of political depravity!

And Bill not only gave us respectability; he gave us a family tree. We used to go back only to John C. Fremont, but now we go clear back to Lazarus!

This righteousness has had a wonderful effect on Republicans down home. They go around, wrapped in a mantle of iridescent exaltation, a fine frenzy of consecration, shading off into a determination, as sublime as it is severe, a determination to lead cold, drab lives of self-denial.

We are mighty proud of Bill. There is absolutely nothing the people would not give him — unless they wanted it themselves.

It is strange that he ever succeeded in politics; he took but little interest in it for years and did not begin to vote till well past sixteen. He started as a poll-book holder and in the great fight just ended this Little Hoosier Giant held the United States between his thumb and first finger just as lightly and just as blandly and just as confidently as he held that first poll-book.

And he has been able to grow in fame and not outgrow his millinery. When they took his measure for a halo it was found to be identical with that of the old slouch hat he used to wear while trying lawsuits before a justice of the peace!

He has never been able to forget that he is a Republican. That's a horrible thing to contemplate, but it's so. If Bill had been on the Ark, he would have given the Elephant the first stateroom and thrown the Jackass overboard!

If Bill's your friend, he'll get you out of jail, and the ability to radiate this assurance has been a priceless asset to him in politics!

And he is broad. In the late campaign he was broad enough to let us Progressives work our heads off for his Standpat zoological garden and he has been able to keep his face straight up to the present moment.

As a harmonizer he beats the world. He can make the other fellow furnish all of the harmony and then choke up as he wonders if he hasn't been a little bit too hard on Bill.

I shall always regret that Bill didn't represent us at the Paris Peace Conference. He would have made two or three swift passes — and those hostile nations would have fallen into such violent love-making that it would have been necessary to pull down the blinds!

Chauncey M. Depew presents
William Jennings Bryan

On February 27, 1922, a joint meeting of all the Protestant churches of St. Augustine, Florida, was held for the purpose of hearing William Jennings Bryan deliver his lecture against Darwin's theory of evolution. Bryan (1860–1925), the "Great Commoner" and one of the most unsuccessful great leaders in American political history, was introduced on this occasion by Chauncey Depew, lawyer, railroad executive, and orator of consummate skill.

It is a great pleasure for me to perform this very agreeable duty of introducing to you your distinguished guest and my friend, the Honorable William Jennings Bryan. While we differ radically in politics, I have a high regard and great respect for him. He has been prominent in so many fields and discussed so many questions, and is such a many-sided man, that there are issues upon which we can occupy the same platform. I am twenty-eight years older than my friend, but he is an iconoclast; that is, idol smasher. I have never been able to influence his public opinion or politics.

I first met Mr. Bryan at the Republican National Convention at St. Louis, where Mr. McKinley was nominated for the first time. Mr. Bryan was there as a reporter for a Democratic newspaper in Omaha, and I was there as a delegate from the state of New York. I have met Mr. Bryan in the same capacity at every Republican convention since. He attends our conventions as a representative of the press, and as such learns the interior machinery, the motives, and the powers which produce results. With this information, he goes as a delegate to the Democratic conventions and controls their nominations and dictates the platform.

The dramatic situation is history and the fortunes of parties which make history are always exceedingly interesting. I know of nothing more picturesque or more remarkable than the appearance of Mr. Bryan, six weeks after the Republican convention at St. Louis, as a delegate at the Democratic convention at Chicago. This was a body of very able and experienced men. Very few of them knew Mr. Bryan, who appeared among them as a young man, unknown in public life or party councils. It is often claimed, and the claim frequently emphasized, that the day of the orator has passed. It is said that the newspaper has destroyed his power and influence, but the most extraordinary refutation of this statement was in the action of that convention under the influence of a speech by Mr. Bryan. After days of exhaustive discussion by the leaders of the party, this young man went to the platform and electrified both the delegates and the spectators. His eloquence completely swept them off their feet. All other candidates were laid aside, and the convention, with unanimity and enthusiasm, nominated him for President. In that speech was this phrase: "You shall not press down upon the brow of labor this crown of thorns; you shall not crucify mankind upon a cross of gold." The sentiment and its picturesque clothing struck the popular imagination. It was reproduced in every newspaper in the country and many abroad.

Very few men are able to capitalize their defeat. It usually produces a paralysis of hope and stupefies ambition, but this young orator arose phoenix-like from the ashes of his campaign. He entered the journalistic field and established the *Commoner*.

I recall that in one of his campaigns, I was assigned to follow him in his tour of New York and speak after he had left in the same places and to the same audiences. At one of these towns, there was an interval of several hours after he had left and I arrived. There was no Prohibition amendment in those days, nor Volstead Act, and in this town every saloon was licensed. A holiday and a waiting crowd under such circumstances gave me an audience so highly fortified with mountain whiskey, that it was an unruly mob. They roared, they shouted, and made speech impossible. There was at that time a violent controversy as to whether it was Admiral Sampson or Admiral Schley who had won the battle of Santiago. For no reason, except a singular eccentricity of the public mind, the controversy assumed a political aspect. When the crowd became quiet for a moment, because of exhaustion, I shouted to them, "You are trying to suppress free speech with the weapon with which Sampson (sic) slew the Philistines." An athletic citizen jumped in the air and shouted so that you could hear him a mile, "That is another Republican lie. It was not Sampson, it was Schley."

Our friend has not only been nominated three times for the presidency, and received each time many millions of votes, he has done more. The magazines are full now of reminiscences and autobiographies in which the authors claim that they created Woodrow Wilson. But, my friends, except for the power, the influence upon his fellow delegates, the management and eloquence of Mr. Bryan, Woodrow Wilson would not have been nominated for the presidency, and that nomination gave him his opportunity.

Many college professors and brilliant writers are presenting volumes and articles in the magazines to prove that, as a result of the primary in elections, and because of the indifference of the people who will not take an interest in the primary, the bosses have got control of its machinery and have filled Congress with second-rate men. Now every right-thinking citizen wants not only his own party, but the opposite party, to be represented in the Senate and the House of Representatives by the best representatives. Mr. Bryan has become a citizen of the state of Florida. It is as a citizen of this growing and most promising commonwealth he is here with us tonight. If he should happily be chosen to represent Florida, this fine state would always have, during his incumbency of office, the first page in the press of the country. Ladies and Gentlemen, I have the pleasure of presenting to you the Honorable William Jennings Bryan.

Helen H. Waller *presents*

Estes Kefauver

By conventional standards, Estes Kefauver (1903–1963) had everything against him in seeking the Democratic senatorial nomination in Tennessee in 1948 — a liberal voting record in the House, the opposition of a powerful state political machine, and a name difficult to pronounce. The fact that he won gave progressive groups everywhere a much-needed shot in the arm. At the eighteenth annual forum of the *New York Herald Tribune*, October 25, 1949, Mr. Kefauver was introduced by the presiding chairman and forum director, Mrs. Helen H. Waller.

SOME TIME the peculiar alchemy of the American electoral process may produce a southern President. Our next speaker is the prototype of the kind of southern liberal that is certain to play an increasingly important role in the national political scene. Estes Kefauver is a southerner whose liberalism makes him representative of the new South. He served for ten years as a member of the House of Representatives prior to his spectacular triumph over the Crump machine in the 1948 senatorial elections. His name stands for many of the programs and policies which are helping to keep our democracy competitive in this increasingly complex world. He has been a staunch supporter of the Tennessee Valley Authority and now advocates the application of the regional principle to the Columbia River Valley. He is among the most influential proponents of congressional reform. He has been the Senate leader of the movement for a federal union of the democracies. We are privileged to have this distinguished legislator with us tonight. Senator Estes Kefauver.

W. Randolph Burgess presents
Paul H. Douglas

Paul H. Douglas, Senator from Illinois (1949–1967), was introduced at the April 26, 1950, meeting of the Academy of Political Science by W. Randolph Burgess, banker and chairman of the executive committee of the National City Bank of New York.

IN JANUARY 1949, in the halls of Congress, there was a sudden stir. Something unusual had happened, and those best able to know traced it down to the coming of a Lochinvar out of the West. The interesting thing was that he did not really come out of the West, although people thought he did; he came from Salem, Massachusetts, where he was born, and he went to Bowdoin, where he played football and debated and was Phi Beta Kappa. And then — General Eisenhower, you are partly responsible for him, because he came here, to Columbia, to study, and took his master's degree. After wandering about some little time teaching in various institutions, he came back and took his doctor's degree. So the responsibility is complete. Then he went to the University of Chicago, and over a period of years did an exceedingly competent job in analyzing labor statistics, unemployment, social security. He served several tours of duty in Washington, but established himself in that field as a man who is respected.

Then politics interested him, and in 1939 he became an alderman of the city of Chicago. There are many interesting stories about that, but I am not going to try to tell them, because I do not know them well enough.

At fifty years of age, in 1942, he enlisted as a private in the Marines. He went abroad, was wounded in combat, became a lieutenant colonel. And whatever else he may do, we take our hats off to a man who, at fifty years of age, goes through that experience.

Then he defeated for the Senate the redoubtable "Curley" Brooks. More than that, he has been the chairman of a Subcommittee on Monetary Policy of the Committee on Economic Report. As one of the victims who was called before that Committee, I want to say that Paul Douglas gave a fair hearing, a careful hearing, and a penetrating hearing, on that subject. The small document that has been published as the report of that Committee is, in my judgment, one of the landmarks in the understanding of the monetary policy of this country, and has had an important influence already in shaping our monetary policy.

In the last few days you saw that Senator Douglas had the courage, in facing a bill on public works, to say, "This is pork. This must be cut." And that takes courage.

I do not know whether any of you read in the *Herald Tribune* for April 19, in the column written by Mr. McConnell, that it would take about a five-million-dollar appropriation for Chicago to build a canal that would connect the city with the Mississippi. Senator Douglas went home and told his people in Chicago that, while he believed in that proposal, it was not timely to ask for it now, and he would not vote for it now.

I have a great pleasure in introducing to you Senator Paul H. Douglas.

Thomas W. Lamont presents

W. L. Mackenzie King

W. L. Mackenzie King, Prime Minister of Canada (1921–1930 and 1935–1948), was introduced at a dinner in his honor December 2, 1942, by Thomas W. Lamont, partner of J. P. Morgan and Company and chairman of the executive committee of the Pilgrims of the United States.

I WOULD have you know that though this is a highly honorable body, our occasions are informal. We say just about whatever we please, whether it be on the record or off the record, and this leads me quite naturally to read you a telegram of regret from Sir Ronald Campbell, one of the Ministers in your Embassy, Lord Halifax, and, subsequently, the Dominion Prime Minister's comment upon it:

Very much regret shall be unable to attend Pilgrims' Dinner tonight as shall be detained by duties in Washington. Please convey to the President of the Pilgrims and to Mrs. Mackenzie King my deep regrets.

RONALD CAMPBELL

I handed that to the Prime Minister to read, and he said, "I have been looking for her all my life, but I haven't found her yet."

The Prime Minister also reminded me, although it is in *Who's Who*, which I have studied very diligently for the last few days, that he was born in Canada, in a town at that time that was called Berlin. When World War No. 1 broke out, the name was very properly changed to Kitchener. And I wonder if you recall, Mr. Prime Minister, how Lord Kitchener, as Minister of War in the early years in the last great struggle, was frequently accused by his fellow members in the Cabinet, as often happens I understand, of not revealing sufficiently to them his war strategy, whereupon he retorted, "Well, what would you expect? Two thirds of my Cabinet are married men!"

233

I say this with due respect to our fair friends in the gallery who, I am sure, are most discreet.

You know, Mr. Prime Minister, I feel that we in America have a right to envy Canada in more aspects than one, and before entering upon the serious business of the evening, I might mention one or two of these points, the first of which is serious. It relates back to the time of the great depression, from 1929 on, for several years. I do not like to recall that period, but I have to say this in behalf of Canada, that while here in the United States we were closing ten thousand banks, and while our American depositors were losing sums of money that I should hesitate to recall in this cheerful assemblage, there wasn't a single bank closed in all Canada; there was no bank holiday, and, moreover, there wasn't a single dollar lost by a depositor in the Canadian banks — a very great record.

Now, Mr. Prime Minister, another matter which may not seem to you important, but figured somewhat in our scheme of things — we have heard a good deal of late about the Four Freedoms, or perhaps the Five Freedoms. The Sixth Freedom hasn't been mentioned so much, freedom to eat and to drink what we please! You have always had that; we have not always had that. In fact, looking even to our neighbor to the south, which is quite a different proposition from our neighbor to the north, I must recall that twenty years ago, during that glad period of our "noble experiment," I had to go to Mexico on a semi-official mission. The genial President Obregón asked me to come and see him with my staff immediately, and as soon as I arrived in the spacious chamber, its walls lined with ancient Spanish and Mexican trappings, the President rang for servants and said to them, "Bring wine, bring whiskey, bring brandy, bring liqueurs of all kinds." And then he turned to me with a charming smile and said, "Mr. Lamont, I want you to know that at last you are in a free country." ...

Now, to be somewhat more serious, Mr. Prime Minister, I should like to speak to you and to the Pilgrims for a moment or two of one of the fresh symbols of friendship that has always existed between Canada and the United States of America.

On November 21 last there was opened for traffic the great

Alaska Highway, a Northwest Passage far more realistic than that which the ancient mariners sought to find centuries ago. The dedication of this route was one of the most significant events of Canadian-American relations of all time. The enterprise was a great adventure in which your people, Mr. Prime Minister, and our own, shared. As one of your Cabinet Ministers, Ian MacKenzie, declared, "Canada provided the soil while the United States provided the toil."

As in every vital achievement of man, there was romance as well as dogged toil and hardihood in it all. Can you not see the picture: Workmen felling the giant trees, hewing through mountain passes, casting bridges over the rushing torrents? With the brief northern summer wearing away and the days growing shorter, the task became ever more strenuous but neither icy winds nor swollen streams gave pause to these sturdy pioneers of progress. Working swiftly through the fading wintry twilights, it was only ten days ago that they came out from the rush of ageless rivers to the shadows of the towering Alaskan peaks, and there in the silence of the snow-clad spruces completed their monumental task....

And now on the personal side, Mr. Mackenzie King, it is a great satisfaction to all of us American Pilgrims that, after your college studies at the University of Toronto were completed, you came first to Chicago University for your early studies in economics, and then went to Harvard, where for three years you were a fellow in political science, and won a traveling fellowship for work in that field. That is a matter of great gratification to us and to all our educators in America.

If one is truly a liberal and desires democratic freedom, one has to do something about it. Mr. Mackenzie King is one who has always done something about it. For over forty years he has been in the public life of Canada. This is his twenty-fourth year as leader of his party, and he has served as Prime Minister longer than any other statesman in the whole British Commonwealth.

And so, as I present him to you, and I can say that we, like his own countrymen, can be proud of him as the worthy leader of our great neighbor; proud of him as a liberal statesman who, in office and out, has always worked for progressive ideas; proud of him as the man who within ten days of the time when Britain declared war in September 1939, unified and took his own country to fight by Britain's side; proud of him as the leader who, when France fell in 1940, rushed across the seas to England all that Canada had in fighting men, air men, equipment, munitions, transport — stripping Canada to help Britain, then fighting in her superb spirit and valor to stave off the Hitler invasion.

Finally, we can be glad and proud to welcome him here tonight as our comrade and our friend. I ask the Pilgrims to rise and give greeting to the Prime Minister of the Dominion of Canada.

Joseph A. Choate presents

James Bryce

British historian and diplomat, and author of *The American Common-wealth*, James Bryce (1838–1922) became Ambassador to the United States in 1907 and was welcomed to his new post by the distinguished American lawyer and diplomat Joseph H. Choate at a dinner given by the Pilgrims in New York, March 23, 1907.

It is a most pleasant duty that has been entrusted to me, to propose the health of His Excellency, the British Ambassador, and I shall endeavor to do it briefly and pertinently. I shall indulge in no abstractions. I shall say nothing tonight of "hands across the sea." Partly because I have exhausted myself on that sentiment on many former occasions, and because that delightful but somewhat threadbare sentiment has been entrusted to another speaker, who will bring to it all the freshness of novelty and will sing that favorite old song to an entirely new hymn. Neither shall I venture to say anything about our common language, our common history and our common literature; nor will I claim any ownership in our Chaucer, our Shakespeare and our Milton, because I do not venture to encroach upon the province — the peculiar province — of the distinguished guest of the evening.

I know very well that a living ambassador in actual service, even he, has rights — rights that ex-officios and back numbers are bound to respect. I speak not for myself only, but for these numerous back numbers and ex-officios who are about me on either side — Governor Morton, General Porter, and Mr. Shaw, and last, though not least, Senator Spooner. We are all ex-officios and back numbers. We are really as good as dead, although we don't want to have that fact generally known.

Now, let me say a little about Mr. Bryce in the concrete and not wander off into these diversions, which might amuse you but would give you little light on the man that we are met to honor. I can appeal to a close and long-abiding friendship with our honored guest — six years of intimate association with him, in which my regard and affection for him were constantly growing. I remember also that he was among the first to greet me when I landed in England, and the last to bid me farewell when I left. It would be strange indeed if I did not take great delight in this opportunity of presenting him on this first occasion of his appearance as an ambassador before a public audience in America. I confess that long before I knew Mr. Bryce I was very much attached to him. I had a very ardent sympathy for him as a brother lawyer, and there are a great many in this room who know how close that tie is. The tie of the lawyer to the lawyer is close, although perhaps the tie of the lawyer to the client, or the client to the lawyer, is a little closer.

Now, in the year 1862, Mr. Bryce was admitted at Lincoln's Inn as a student of the common law — Lincoln's Inn, one of those grand old nurseries of the law and cradles of liberty; and he must have had a very, very long legal lineage, for I find on the same register that another James Bryce — if it was another — a man of exactly the same name, James Bryce, was admitted at the same Inn nearly four hundred years before, in 1478 — fourteen years before Columbus discovered America. Now, think how far back he traces his legal line. You remember Dr. Holmes' answer to the anxious mother, that asked him how early a boy's education should begin. He said, "Why, ma'am, at least two hundred years before he was born." But this man has had four hundred years of nurture and training in the law. What the Tudors planted and watered found its full fruition in the glorious reign of Victoria and of Edward VII. And who can wonder that, with such nurture and such origin, he has such extreme felicity in the handling of great social and constitutional and legal questions and knows our history all by heart?

To have practiced at the Bar of England, as our friend has for fifteen years, is a great education in itself, as I personally know. To have been for twenty-three years Regius Professor of Civil Law at Oxford surely was a sure foundation for the success that has followed him as statesman, as author, and as citizen of the world. Certainly no more wholesome training could be had for public life in which he has been engaged, and for the many great offices which he has filled with so much distinction. Our whole experience shows that the law is the true entrance and avenue to public and political life. It was not always so, even in America — today the paradise of lawyers, and which everybody, from the President down, seems to be doing his best to make more and more of a paradise for them. I say it was not always so, even in America, because in the good old colony days of New England there were no such things as professional advocates, and when John Locke, the celebrated philosopher, made his famous constitution for the Carolinas he expressly provided that there should be no lawyers and that nobody should plead for a fee. And in order to make sure that the constitution and the laws should be protected by the total absence of lawyers, he further provided — and I call Mr. Bryce's especial attention to this — that there should never be any comments or criticisms upon constitutions or laws, so that they might be perfectly easy and plain to be understood by everybody. Now, I would like to know what would have become of Mr. Bryce or myself if the constitution of Locke had continued in force until this day? I am afraid neither of us would have made any considerable progress; but fortunately we have outgrown the wisdom of the philosophers, and I think that Mr. Bryce will agree with me in advising all aspiring young men of the English-speaking race that if they hope ever to become ambassadors from either half of it to the other they shall begin by the study and the practice of the English law.

Well, now, we are under a tremendous debt of gratitude for the splendid gift that he gave us. I suppose you would like it better if I should state exactly what that gift was. It was a very rare gift. It was a gift that so wise a man as Robert Burns seemed to have doubted whether it could ever be given to anybody, for it was his constant and never-failing prayer:

> O wad some Power the giftie gie us
> To see oursels as others see us!

Joseph A. Choate presents James Bryce   239

And that is exactly what Mr. Bryce gave us now nearly fifteen —
yes, eighteen — years ago.

I believe it was Dean Swift who said that the man who made two
ears of corn grow, or two blades of grass grow, where only one grew
before, would deserve the everlasting gratitude of mankind. But
what are we to say of the man who made all the people of a great
nation think twice as much of themselves as they ever thought before? I believe when he began writing that book his original idea
was to explain us to his own countrymen, but he ended in explain-
ing us to ourselves. And it was a very great service that he did us in
that way. Don't you see the comparison between Christopher Columbus and James Bryce? Christopher Columbus discovered America to all the rest of the world, but Mr. Bryce was the first one who
discovered America to herself. So if we ever think too much of ourselves, as some of his more critical and less indulgent countrymen
are sometimes fond of saying — if we do think too much of ourselves,
it is very largely his fault. It was he that struck the blow that first
inflamed our bump of self-esteem.

I need not tell you how very richly his path has been strewn with
civic wreaths and laurels, or what a commanding place he has taken
among learned and scholarly men — what a great traveler he has
been, how he has permeated the whole of South Africa, what Al-
pine summits he has mastered, how alone he reached the dreary top
of Mount Ararat, seeking for some traces of the Ark and of our origin
and common progenitors; and he has confidentially told me that he
did find a stick of timber on top of Ararat that he thinks might possibly have composed a part of Noah's Ark.

Well, that is not all that can be said about Mr. Bryce, although I
do not want to weary him by expatiating upon his merits. You know
very well how his published studies in history, in literature, in
biography, have enriched our literature, how many universities
have claimed him for their own. Why, it would take from now until
after the hour that the president has assigned for our adjournment
simply to enumerate them. To his own alma mater, Glasgow, you
might add Edinburgh, Aberdeen, St. Andrews, Cambridge, London, Oxford, Budapest, Victoria, Toronto, and I really don't know

how many more. And you know something of the great offices he has filled at home — member of Parliament for I don't know how many years — they never could get him out; and then besides that, he was Under Secretary for Foreign Affairs, President of the Board of Trade, Chancellor of the Duchy of Lancaster, and, last but not least, Chief Secretary for Ireland. I knew him for six years as one of a little band that constituted the forlorn hope of his party for all those years in the House of Commons; but, as Shakespeare says, "the whirligig of Time brings in his reverses" here as well as there, and now he has been taken away from one of the great offices under the British government, and from a great place in the Cabinet to come and fill his post at Washington, which is the crowning honor of them all. . . .

It is nearly a score of years since he produced his book. He will find now great changes have taken place — tremendous developments. Some of the prophecies in which he indulged — for he was a prophet — some of his prophecies have not turned out to be exactly as he thought, but most of them have been strikingly verified, and some of those perils which he foresaw for us in the far distant future are now already upon us. In all our hopes, in all our apprehensions, we may be sure always of his constant sympathy. Let us hope that he may long remain among us, and that both countries together, whose abiding friendship no man can doubt, will by his aid be found working together for the advancement of civilization and justice, and, above all, for the peace of the world. In the coming summer, at The Hague, we are to have a grand opportunity for cooperation in an earnest endeavor to limit the chance of war, to put an end to the relics of barbarism which still disgrace it, to secure the rights of neutrals and to advance the great cause of arbitration and of peace. Let us embrace the opportunity and make the most of it, and I am sure that our distinguished guest will say "Amen!"

Gentlemen, I have now the very great pleasure of presenting to you and asking you to drink his health, His Excellency the Right Honourable James Bryce, the British Ambassador to the United States.

Adlai E. Stevenson presents
Pandit Jawaharlal Nehru

The distinguished 1952 Democratic nominee for President, Governor Adlai E. Stevenson of Illinois, introduced Pandit Nehru (1889–1964), Prime Minister of India, at the Chicago Council of Foreign Relations dinner, October 26, 1951.

WE LIVE in an age swept by tides of history so powerful they shatter human understanding. Only a tiny handful of men have influenced the implacable forces of our time. To this small company of the truly great, our guest on this memorable day in Chicago and Illinois belongs.

He does us honor to come here and we pay him our *homage,* not just because he is the Prime Minister of India, but because he is a great and a good man. Pandit Jawaharlal Nehru belongs to the even *smaller* company of historic figures who wore a halo in their own lifetimes.

"The nation is safe in his hands." Those were Mahatma Gandhi's concluding words when he publicly chose Pandit Nehru as his heir and successor — because of his bravery, his prudence and discipline, his vision and practicality, his humility and purity.

Three hundred and fifty million of his countrymen love him, follow him, bless him for his brilliant leadership in their struggle for independence, and, some say, even more because of his character, spirit, and sacrifice. Long ago he forsook ease and wealth and security, to risk life itself for his country.

A quarter of his life he has spent in prison for the same cause our own revolutionary ancestors pledged their lives, their fortunes, and their sacred honor — freedom. Born to exalted station he knows the "art of being a king," yet he has a common touch that excites the devotion and understanding of all kinds and conditions of people, and he has a pen and tongue that stir the hearts of millions. In his address to Congress he said: "Even when preparing to resist aggression, the objective of peace and reconciliation must never be lost sight of, and heart and mind must be attuned to this supreme aim, and not swayed or clouded by hatred or fear." So spoke our own Abraham Lincoln. These are words we understand, Mr. Prime Minister, and we are grateful for the reminder.

My friends, I bid you mark well what he says to us, for he is the voice of India — the home of a sixth of the human race and the largest stable, solvent democracy in the East. India can be the anchor of freedom in all Asia, but around it swirl dangerous currents and in it live millions in incredible poverty. Bedeviled with the infinite problems of national infancy, of the partition with Pakistan, of welding innumerable classes and minorities into a single Eastern state based on the liberal tradition of the West, his tasks beggar description.

Indeed I must acknowledge Your Excellency a personal debt. Whenever the problems of Illinois get too oppressive I think of India and of you, Sir, and immediately I feel much better! We welcome you to Illinois.

Virgil M. Hancher presents
Eleanor Roosevelt

Anna Eleanor Roosevelt (1884–1962) was introduced to the Adult Education Forum, Des Moines, March 14, 1949, by Virgil M. Hancher, President of the State University of Iowa.

IT IS PROBABLE that few persons in this or any age have touched life at as many points as has Mrs. Roosevelt. She has been the witness of both tragedy and triumph, and has faced each with wisdom and equanimity.

The political party of which her illustrious husband was so long the head has won five consecutive national elections. If one cause more than another can be assigned for that unique record, it is that that party and its leaders convinced large segments of our people that the problems which concerned them in their personal lives were of concern to the party. I venture the prophecy that when the history of our era is written, historians will agree that no one had more to do with the creation of this attitude than had Mrs. Roosevelt.

But her interests transcend our national boundaries, and she has made her contribution to international affairs. We live in fearful and anxious times. To an extraordinary degree our hopes for peace lie in the success of the United Nations. As one of the delegates of the United States to the United Nations, Mrs. Roosevelt has carried into that organization the broad humanitarian interests so characteristic of her efforts within the nation. With her have gone our hopes, and in her efforts we wish her every success.

Ladies and Gentlemen, I have the privilege and honor of presenting to you Mrs. Franklin D. Roosevelt, who will speak on the subject "The Success and Failures of the United Nations."

ACKNOWLEDGMENTS

The compilers wish to express their appreciation to authors, speakers, and publishers who allowed their work to be printed in this book as indicated:

Academy of Political Science for introductions by Lewis Douglas, W. Randolph Burgess, Thomas S. Lamont, and Leon Fraser, which appeared in the Academy's *Proceedings*.

Advertising Club of New York for identifying the occasion and date of the late Gertrude Lawrence's appearance before the Club.

American Academy of Arts and Letters for introductions by William Lyon Phelps and Nicholas Murray Butler which appeared in its *Publication No. 75*, 1931, and for Deems Taylor's presentation of Grace George which appeared in its *Proceedings*, second series, No. 1, 1951.

American Law Institute for introductions by George Wharton Pepper and Harrison Tweed, which appeared in the Institute's *Proceedings*: 1956, pp. 24–25; 1957, pp. 540–42; 1958, pp. 518–19. Copyrighted 1956–58, and reprinted with permission of the American Law Institute.

Dr. Frederick Anderson, editor of the "Mark Twain Papers" for permission to publish Samuel Clemens' introduction of Winston Churchill, reproduced from a unique typescript copy in the "Mark Twain Papers." Other versions have appeared based on contemporary newspaper accounts. The compilers are indebted to John Marshall, librarian at Middle Tennessee State University, for the suggestion of this introduction.

The Bookmark for James L. Godfrey's introduction of Frank Borden Hanes which appeared in *The Bookmark* (Friends of the University of North Carolina), August 1961.

Carnegie Institution of Washington for John Campbell Merriam's introduction of Ray L. Wilbur which appeared in his *Published Papers and Addresses*, published by the Institution in 1938.

Columbia University Forum for Lionel Trilling's introduction of T. S Eliot reprinted from the *Columbia University Forum*, Fall 1958, vol. 2, no. 1. Copyright 1958 by Columbia University.

Dodd, Mead and Company for Owen Seaman's introduction of Stephen Leacock from Leacock's *My Discovery of England*, copyright 1922 by Dodd, Mead and Company, Inc.

245

Economic Club of Detroit for introductions by Jerome P. Cavanagh, Charles T. Fisher, Jr., Henry Ford II, William T. Gossett, and Lee Hills which appeared in the series of *Addresses* presented before and published by the Club.

Economic Club of New York for introductions by Alfred Hayes, John G. Milburn, Juan T. Trippe, Arthur K. Watson, and William R. Willcox. Published with permission of Dwight Eckerman, Executive Director, Economic Club of New York.

Executive Club of Chicago for introductions by Thomas H. Coulter, Richard T. Cragg, Chester Davis, Donald J. Erickson, John C. Lewe, Harold O. McLain, Thomas R. Mulroy, and James E. Day, which appeared in the *Executives' Club News*.

George C. Marshall Research Foundation for the text and permission to publish Harry S. Truman's introduction of George C. Marshall in the Marshall papers of the Foundation.

George Washington University Press for Chauncey Depew's introduction of William Jennings Bryan from William H. Yeager's *Chauncey Mitchell Depew — Orator*, published by the George Washington University Press, 1934.

Harper and Brothers, Publishers, for Samuel L. Clemens' introduction of Joseph B. Hawley which appeared in *Mark Twain: A Biography* by Albert Bigelow Paine. Copyright 1912 by Harper and Brothers; copyright 1940, by Dora L. Paine; Samuel L. Clemens' introduction of Henry M. Stanley which appeared in *Mark Twain's Speeches*, introduction by Albert Bigelow Paine, copyright 1923, 1950, vol. 28, pp. 131–32 of *Mark Twain's Works*. Harper and Row, Publishers, for G. Lynn Sumner's introduction of Dr. Victor Heiser which appeared in *We Have With Us Tonight*, copyright 1941 by Harper and Row, Publishers, Inc.

Houghton Mifflin Company for Will Rogers' introduction of Franklin D. Roosevelt which appeared in *The Autobiography of Will Rogers*, selected and edited by Donald Day, copyright 1949 by Houghton Mifflin Company; for Walter P. Webb's introduction of Harry S. Truman which appeared in Webb's *An Honest Preface and Other Essays*, copyright 1959 by the Riverside Press, Cambridge.

Indiana Society of Chicago for Frederick Landis' introduction of Will H. Hays which appeared in the Indiana Society Yearbook, 1921.

George Jessel for his introductions of Jack Benny and Groucho Marx which appeared in his book *You Too Can Make a Speech*, published in 1940 by the Grayson Publishing Corporation.

Life Insurance Association of America for the introduction of Edward Duffield by Job E. Hedges which appeared in the Association of Life Insurance Presidents, Proceedings, December 6–7, 1923.

The Lotos Club, for introductions of Roger Stevens and Maxwell D. Taylor by Howard S. Cullman and Francis Cardinal Spellman which appeared in the Lotos Leaf, January and February 1966. Printed with permission of John G. Brunini, Executive Director, Lotos Club, New York.

The Middle States Association of Colleges and Secondary Schools for Canon Martin's introduction of McGeorge Bundy which appeared in its Proceedings, 80th Convention, December 1–3, 1966.

National Book League, London, for Robert Lusty's introduction of Sir Norman Birkett from his The Use and Abuse of Reading, published by the Cambridge University Press.

National Education Association of the United States for introductions by Joseph M. Gwinn, Henry Hill, and Martha A. Shull in the 1928, 1944, and 1957 N.E.A. Addresses and Proceedings.

New York Herald Tribune for Helen Waller's introductions of Estes Kefauver and Bertrand Russell which appeared in the 18th and 20th Annual Forum on Current Problems, published by the New York Herald Tribune; for Mrs. William B. Meloney's introduction of Dorothy Thompson which appeared in the 5th Annual Forum on Current Problems, published by the New York Herald Tribune.

The Newcomen Society in North America for the introduction of Norman S. Marshall by Arthur B. Langlie which appeared in the Newcomen Society pamphlet The Salvation Army, 1960.

Louis Nizer for his introductions of Harry W. Chase, Albert Einstein, and Grover Whalen which appeared in his book Thinking on Your Feet, copyright 1940 by Liveright Publishing Corporation; to Liveright, Publishers, New York, N.Y. for introductions of Heywood Broun and George Gershwin from Thinking On Your Feet by Louis Nizer. Rev. ed. copyright 1963.

Pilgrims of the United States for introductions by John W. Davis, Thomas W. Lamont, and Hugh Bullock which appeared in the Pilgrim's Publication Speeches at Dinner for 1942, 1951, 1963.

Prentice-Hall, Inc. for Professor R. Spencer's introduction of Anne O'Hare McCormick which appeared in William H. Yeager's Effective Speaking for Every Occasion, 2nd Edition, © 1951. Reprinted by permission of Prentice-Hall, Inc., Englewood Cliffs, New Jersey.

Science for Warren Weaver's introduction of Sir Charles Percy Snow, which appeared in *Science*, CXXXIII (January 27, 1961), pp. 255–62. Copyright 1961 by the American Association for the Advancement of Science.

Society of Authors, 84 Drayton Gardens, London, for permission to use the prologue by George Bernard Shaw from the screen version of *Major Barbara*.

Texas Law Review for D. A. Simmons' introduction of Walter S. Fenton which appeared in the *Texas Law Review*, October 1939.

West Publishing Company for Joseph H. Choate's introduction of James Bryce which appeared in Choate's *Arguments and Addresses of Joseph Hodges Choate* collected and edited by Frederick C. Hicks, published by the West Publishing Company, 1926.

And to Everett M. Dirksen (presenting Robert A. Taft), Harry S. Ashmore (J. William Fulbright), Robert J. Blakely (Stephen Hayes Bush), Lucile Nix (Edmon Low), Rose Z. Sellers (Harry D. Gideonse), Hedley Donovan (Henry Luce), Melvin Brorby (Arnold J. Toynbee), John E. Stipp (Nathan M. Pusey), John G. Buchanan (Augustus N. Hand), Frank P. Graham (Robert M. Hutchins), Clare E. Griffin (James Palmer), Virgil M. Hancher (Franklyn Bliss Snyder, Eleanor Roosevelt), John Adams Lowe (E. J. Pratt), Thomas W. Martin (Charles F. Kettering), William Clarke Mason (George Wharton Pepper), Edgar L. Schnadig (Gerald Wendt), Adlai E. Stevenson (Pandit Nehru), W. O. DuVall (Billy Graham), and the Rev. Msgr. W. E. Croarkin (Archbishop O'Brien, Rabbi Frank F. Rosenthal).

INDEX

I. Persons Making Introductions

II.   Persons Introduced